Microwave Magic
Beef II

Grolier Limited
TORONTO

Contributors to this series:

Recipes and Technical Assistance:
École de cuisine Bachand-Bissonnette
Cooking consultants:
Denis Bissonette
Michèle Émond
Dietician:
Christiane Barbeau
Photos:
Laramée Morel Communications
Audio-Visuelles
Design:
Claudette Taillefer
Assistants:
Julie Deslauriers
Philippe O'Connor
Joan Pothier
Accessories:
Andrée Cournoyer
Writing:
Communications La Griffe Inc.
Text Consultants:
Cap et bc inc.
Advisors:
Roger Aubin
Joseph R. De Varennes
Gaston Lavoie
Kenneth H. Pearson

Assembly:
Carole Garon
Vital Lapalme
Jean-Pierre Larose
Carl Simmons
Gus Soriano
Marc Vallières
Production Managers:
Gilles Chamberland
Ernest Homewood
Production Assistants:
Martine Gingras
Catherine Gordon
Kathy Kishimoto
Peter Thomlison
Art Director:
Bernard Lamy
Editors:
Laurielle Ilacqua
Susan Marshall
Margaret Oliver
Robin Rivers
Lois Rock
Jocelyn Smyth
Donna Thomson
Dolores Williams
Development:
Le Groupe Polygone Éditeurs Inc.

We wish to thank the following firms, PIER I IMPORTS and LE CACHE POT, for their contribution to the illustration of this set.

Canadian Cataloguing in Publication Data

Main entry under title:

Beef II

(Microwave magic ; 8)
Translation of: Le Boeuf II.
Includes index.
ISBN 0-7172-2429-5

1. Cookery (Beef).   2. Microwave cookery.
I. Series: Microwave magic (Toronto, Ont.) ; 8.

TX832.B8413 1988   641.6'62   C88-094207-X

Contents

Microwave Magic is a multi-volume set, with each volume devoted to a particular type of cooking. So, if you are looking for a chicken recipe, you simply go to one of the two volumes that deal with poultry. Each volume has its own index, and the final volume contains a general index to the complete set.

Microwave Magic puts over twelve hundred recipes at your fingertips. You will find it as useful as the microwave oven itself. Enjoy!

Note from the Editor

How to Use this Book
The books in this set have been designed to make your job as easy as possible. As a result, most of the recipes are set out in a standard way.

We suggest that you begin by consulting the information chart for the recipe you have chosen. You will find there all the information you need to decide if you are able to make it: preparation time, cost per serving, level of difficulty, number of calories per serving and other relevant details. Thus, if you have only 30 minutes in which to prepare the evening meal, you will quickly be able to tell which recipe is possible and suits your schedule.

The list of ingredients is always clearly separated from the main text. When space allows, the ingredients are shown together in a photograph so that you can make sure you have them all without rereading the list—

another way of saving your valuable time. In addition, for the more complex recipes we have supplied photographs of the key stages involved either in preparation or serving.

All the dishes in this book have been cooked in a 700 watt microwave oven. If your oven has a different wattage, consult the conversion chart that appears on the following page for cooking times in different types of oven. We would like to emphasize that the cooking times given in the book are a minimum. If a dish does not seem to be cooked enough, you may return it to the oven for a few more minutes. Also, the cooking time can vary according to your ingredients: their water and fat content, thickness, shape and even where they come from. We have therefore left a blank space on each recipe page in which you can note

the cooking time that suits you best. This will enable you to add a personal touch to the recipes that we suggest and to reproduce your best results every time.

Although we have put all the technical information together at the front of this book, we have inserted a number of boxed entries called **MICROTIPS** throughout to explain particular techniques. They are brief and simple, and will help you obtain successful results in your cooking.

With the very first recipe you try, you will discover just how simple microwave cooking can be and how often it depends on techniques you already use for cooking with a conventional oven. If cooking is a pleasure for you, as it is for us, it will be all the more so with a microwave oven. Now let's get on with the food.

The Editor

Key to the Symbols
For ease of reference, the following symbols have been used on the recipe information charts.

The pencil symbol ✏️🍎 is a reminder to write your cooking time in the space provided.

Level of Difficulty

🍴 Easy

🍴🍴 Moderate

🍴🍴🍴 Complex

Cost per Serving

$ Inexpensive

$ $ Moderate

$ $ $ Expensive

Power Levels

All the recipes in this book have been tested in a 700 watt oven. As there are many microwave ovens on the market with different power levels, and as the names of these levels vary from one manufacturer to another, we have decided to give power levels as a percentage. To adapt the power levels given here, consult the chart opposite and the instruction manual for your oven.

Generally speaking, if you have a 500 watt or 600 watt oven you should increase cooking times by about 30% over those given, depending on the actual length of time required. The shorter the original cooking time, the greater the percentage by which it must be lengthened. The 30% figure is only an average. Consult the chart for detailed information on this topic.

Power Levels

HIGH: 100% - 90%	Vegetables (except boiled potatoes and carrots) Soup Sauce Fruits Browning ground beef Browning dish Popcorn
MEDIUM HIGH: 80% - 70%	Rapid defrosting of precooked dishes Muffins Some cakes Hot dogs
MEDIUM: 60% - 50%	Cooking tender meat Cakes Fish Seafood Eggs Reheating Boiled potatoes and carrots
MEDIUM LOW: 40%	Cooking less tender meat Simmering Melting chocolate
DEFROST: 30% **LOW: 30% - 20%**	Defrosting Simmering Cooking less tender meat
WARM: 10%	Keeping food warm Allowing yeast dough to rise

Cooking Time Conversion Chart

700 watts	600 watts*
5 s	11 s
15 s	20 s
30 s	40 s
45 s	1 min
1 min	1 min 20 s
2 min	2 min 40 s
3 min	4 min
4 min	5 min 20 s
5 min	6 min 40 s
6 min	8 min
7 min	9 min 20 s
8 min	10 min 40 s
9 min	12 min
10 min	13 min 30 s
20 min	26 min 40 s
30 min	40 min
40 min	53 min 40 s
50 min	66 min 40 s
1 h	1 h 20 min

* There is very little difference in cooking times between 500 watt ovens and 600 watt ovens.

Beef: A Long History

Beef plays such an important part in our diet today that it is hard to imagine a time when beef cattle were valued more for their strength and stamina as beasts of burden than for the meat they provided. There no doubt was such a time but, in all likelihood, the role of beef as food was even then not negligible. It is known, for instance, that over eighty centuries ago the Turks and Macedonians raised herds of beef cattle for use as food.

Somehow, however, beef has always been more than a meat —at least in the western world. The whole mythology of the North American West centers on it, as the very word *cowboy* readily attests. Is it possible to mention England without conjuring up a vision of a juicy roast beef with Yorkshire pudding, or the United States without hamburgers or western Canada without T-bone steaks? And can anyone imagine a trip to Paris that does not include a *steak-frites* at some small neighborhood restaurant or bistro?

Given the widespread use of beef and the refinements that have been brought to its cooking over the centuries, it is not surprising that we now have countless ways of preparing it. To accommodate the overwhelming range and variety of recipes for cooking the many cuts of beef, *Microwave Magic* is devoting a second volume to beef cookery. In it you will find new ways of preparing various cuts, many suggestions for sauces that enhance the flavor of beef in unique ways and finally a complete dinner party menu. You will also find in these pages a few recipes for frequently neglected organ meats such as heart, kidney and tongue. As you will discover, these often misunderstood items can provide delightful taste treats.

The first few pages of this book briefly review general information about beef and the main techniques of storing, defrosting and cooking it. For more detailed information, please refer to Volume I of *Microwave Magic*.

All that remains is for us to wish you much enjoyment and success with the recipes that we herewith take pleasure in offering you.

Cuts of Beef

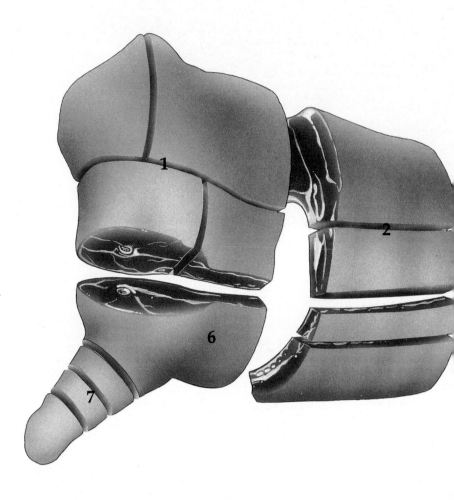

1. Shoulder (Chuck)
Medium and less tender cuts, requiring slow, moist cooking: stews and braised dishes.

2. Rib (Standing rib roast, rib steaks)
Tenderness varies with the specific cut. The upper part provides tender roasting cuts, which are sometimes braised, as well as good steaks. The lower part is suitable for braising and stewing.

3. Loin (T-bone, tenderloin, sirloin)
Very tender cuts for roasts and steaks.

4. Hip (Rump, round, sirloin tip)
Medium and less tender cuts for roasting and braising.

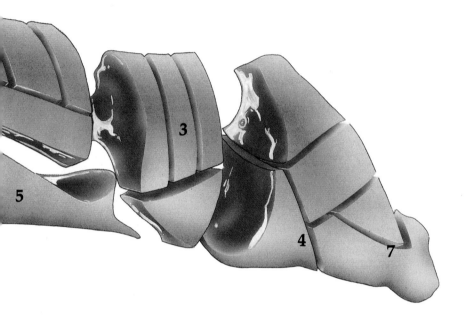

5. Flank
A less tender cut that is usually braised but can be grilled if marinated to soften the fibers.

6. Brisket
A less tender cut that requires slow, moist cooking: braised dishes, stews and corned beef.

7. Shank
A less tender cut for braising and stewing. Because of their marrow content, shank bones are particularly good for making stock for soups and sauces.

Beef and the Microwave Oven

For the modern family, the benefits of defrosting and cooking in the microwave are many. Not only does this new technology save precious time, it also ensures the preservation of natural flavors. However, in order to take full advantage of these benefits, you must observe a few simple rules both in defrosting and cooking. As you will see, these are not particularly onerous; on the contrary, they will, in the end, make meal preparation a great deal easier.

Defrosting

Whether you are dealing with a roast, steaks, ground beef or cubes of stewing beef (see the chart opposite for a guide to defrosting times), the basic principles of defrosting are the same and are very simple. Moreover, the microwaves act in exactly the same way whether you are defrosting or cooking; the microwaves penetrate the food and cause the movement of the molecules to accelerate. When this happens, the molecules bounce and rub against one another, which raises the internal temperature of the food. During the defrosting process, the temperature rises gradually until the food is thawed. Then the cooking process proper begins.

In most microwave ovens, energy is not evenly distributed. As well, many intrinsic characteristics of a particular piece of meat (fat content, the presence of bones, variations in thickness) can affect microwave action in such a way that one part of a steak, for example, could still be rare when the rest of it is well done—a less than satisfactory situation.

There are, however, ways of minimizing the effect of this uneven distribution of microwave energy. As the intensity of the microwaves is lowest in the center of the oven, meat should be arranged so that its thicker parts are at the edge of the cooking dish. Placing bony or fatty parts, which attract the microwaves, in the center will slow down the defrosting of these parts. Also, in order to allow the internal temperature of the meat to even out, it is advisable to divide the defrosting time into short periods interspersed with periods of standing time, each one equal to about one-quarter of the total defrosting time.

As well, you should make sure that no part of the meat is in contact with the juices that seep out during defrosting. Any such part would defrost more quickly and might even begin cooking prematurely. We therefore recommend that you place meat on a rack for defrosting or, if you do not have a microwave-safe rack, on an upside-down plate or saucer in a larger cooking dish.

Defrosting Guide for Cuts of Different Weights

Cut	Defrosting Time at 50%	Defrosting Time at 25%
Rib, rump, eye of round, sirloin tip	12 to 14 min/kg (5-1/2 to 6-1/2 min/lb)	18 to 27 min/kg (9 to 13 min/lb)
Tenderloin, chuck roast, large steaks	7-1/2 to 9-1/2 min/kg (3-1/2 to 4-1/2 min/lb)	15 to 20 min/kg (7 to 9 min/lb)
Small steaks	6-1/2 to 9 min/kg (3 to 4 min/lb)	13 to 18 min/kg (6 to 8 min/lb)
Cubes of beef 2.5 cm (1 inch)	7 to 12 min/kg (3 to 5-1/2 min/lb)	12 to 22 min/kg (5 to 10 min/lb)
Ground beef	7-1/2 to 10 min/kg (3 to 5 min/lb)	12 to 15 min/kg (5 to 7-1/2 min/lb)

* Don't forget to divide the defrosting time into two or three periods in the microwave with periods of standing time equal to a quarter of the total defrosting time in between.

Chart for Cooking Beef

In the case of roasts and irregularly shaped pieces, cover bony, fatty or less meaty parts as well as thinner ends with aluminum foil, which will slow down the action of the microwaves. This is important since fat attracts microwaves and bones reflect them, thereby speeding up the defrosting of the meat next to them.

Defrosting steaks in the microwave is simplicity itself. Place the wrapped steak in the oven. Defrost it until the wrapping can be removed. If at this point any parts of the meat are defrosted, cover these with aluminum foil. Turn the meat over and return to the oven for the second defrosting period. When the time is up, let the meat stand for about 5 minutes. The piece of meat is completely defrosted when you can pierce it with a fork.

Cooking

The amount of time it takes to cook a piece of beef in the microwave oven depends on several factors: the cut, weight, water and fat content and basic tenderness. It will, of course, also vary according to the temperature of the meat when it is put into the oven and the power level at which it is cooked.

Food	Container	Cover	Power Level or Internal Temperature	
Ground beef	casserole	no	100%	1 kg : 8 to 13 min (1 lb : 4 to 6 min) (1-1/2 lb : 7 to 9 min)
Chunks of beef (for simmered dishes or soups)	casserole	yes	50%	1 kg : 45 min (1 lb : 20 min)
Meatballs	round plate or rectangular dish	waxed paper	100%	1 kg : 18 to 28 min (1 lb : 9 to 12 min) (1-1/2 lb : 10 to 13 min)
Meat loaf	round plate or deep rectangular dish	plastic wrap	100% 70% or 75% (170°F) internal temperature	Round loaf: 15 to 20 min Oblong loaf: 17 to 19 min
Braised roasts	rectangular dish or casserole	lid or plastic wrap	50%	43 to 55 min/kg (18 to 23 min/lb)
Stewed beef medium-tender cuts)	casserole	lid or plastic wrap	50%	1 kg : 45 min (1 lb : 20 min)
Tender roasts	rectangular dish with rack		70% very rare: 12 min/kg (5 min/lb) rare: 14 min/kg (6 min/lb) medium: 17 min/kg (7 min/lb) well done: 19 min/kg (8 min/lb) or using temperature probe: very rare: 40°C (100°F) rare: 45°C (110°F) medium rare: 50°C (120°F) well done: 60°C (140°F)	

While cooking times are given for all of the recipes in this book, the chart on page 13 will help you to adapt your favorite conventional recipes to the microwave. Remember as well that you can always check a roast for doneness by piercing it with a fork. If the fork is warm to the touch when you withdraw it and if the juice that seeps out is red, the meat is rare. If, on the other hand, the fork is hot and the juice is pinkish, the meat is medium.

For a more accurate measure, you may use a temperature probe if your oven is equipped with one. Insert the probe into the center of the meat when you put the roast in the oven, and set it for the internal temperature that corresponds to the degree of doneness you want. When the probe shows that the meat has reached that temperature, the oven will automatically turn off.

If you have no temperature probe, you may test for doneness with an ordinary meat thermometer—but only after taking the meat out of the oven. A conventional meat thermometer in an operating microwave oven could cause arcing and seriously damage the oven.

To test braised meat for doneness, pierce with a fork. If the meat is properly done, it will break apart easily. For maximum flavor and juiciness, leave the meat to stand for about 10 minutes before serving.

Converting Your Favorite Recipes

Many people are attracted to new kitchen appliances, buy them and then let them languish unused for fear of the changes they may have to make in their usual way of doing things in order to use them. In actual fact, the adjustments needed are seldom as traumatic as one fears.

You may imagine, for instance, that in order to use a microwave oven you will have to give up your favorite recipes and start collecting a whole new set. Nothing of the sort, however, as you will quickly realize. Most conventional recipes are quite easy to adapt to microwave cooking, with changes that are often minimal. Carefully read the general information on ingredients, techniques, cooking times and utensils, and then study the two Beef Bourguignon recipes that follow. As you will see, there is nothing particularly mysterious involved—nothing at all to intimidate you. You will be a master microwave chef in no time.

Ingredients

Liquids slow down the action of the microwaves, whereas fats speed it up. These ingredients in particular will therefore require adjusting when you are adapting a conventional recipe for the microwave in order to obtain an appropriate balance between the two. (Note the difference in the amount of liquid used in the two recipes on page 15, opposite.)

Techniques

For even cooking it will be necessary to give the dish a half-turn one or more times during the cooking and, in many cases, a period of standing time is required when cooking is complete. To these ends, follow the instructions provided on these points in a microwave recipe similar to the one you wish to adapt.

Cooking Times

It is of course in this regard that a microwave oven offers the greatest advantages. Cooking times for beef will be cut by a third or possibly even by half.

Utensils

Other than metal containers and those with metal trim, any heat-resistant dish—glass or plastic—can be used in the microwave oven.

Beef Bourguignon (in a conventional oven*)

Ingredients

1.1 kg (2-1/2 lb) round steak, cubed
50 mL (1/4 cup) flour
5 mL (1 teaspoon) salt
8 peppercorns, crushed
50 mL (1/4 cup) oil
125 mL (1/2 cup) leeks, sliced
125 mL (1/2 cup) onions, sliced
125 mL (1/2 cup) carrots, thinly sliced
750 mL (1 bottle) dry red wine
30 mL (2 tablespoons) cognac
1 clove garlic, thinly sliced
30 mL (2 tablespoons) parsley, chopped
2 cloves
1 mL (1/4 teaspoon) marjoram
paprika to taste

Method

— In a cup, mix flour, salt and pepper.
— **Heat a frying pan, add the oil and brown the beef cubes.**
— Sprinkle the flour mixture over the beef; mix well. **Transfer to a dutch oven.**
— Add the vegetables and the wine. **Bring to a boil.**
— Heat the cognac, ignite it and pour it over the meat and vegetables. Add seasonings; mix well.
— Cover. **Cook in the oven at 150°C (300°F) or over low heat for 2-1/2 to 3 hours.**
— Serve.

* Steps requiring modification are indicated in bold type.

Beef Bourguignon (in a microwave oven*)

Ingredients

1.1 kg (2-1/2 lb) round steak, cubed
50 mL (1/4 cup) flour
5 mL (1 teaspoon) salt
8 peppercorns, crushed
50 mL (1/4 cup) oil
125 mL (1/2 cup) leeks, sliced
125 mL (1/2 cup) onions, sliced
125 mL (1/2 cup) carrots, thinly sliced
375 mL (1/2 bottle) dry red wine
30 mL (2 tablespoons) cognac
1 clove garlic, thinly sliced
30 mL (2 tablespoons) parsley, chopped
2 cloves
1 mL (1/4 teaspoon) marjoram
paprika to taste

Method

— In a cup, mix flour, salt and pepper.
— **Preheat a browning dish for 7 minutes at 100%; add the oil and sear the beef cubes.**
— Sprinkle the flour mixture over the beef; mix well. **Transfer to a casserole dish if possible.**
— Add the vegetables and the wine. **Cover and cook at 100% for 4 to 5 minutes, or until it reaches a full boil.**
— Heat the cognac, ignite it and pour it over the meat and vegetables. Add seasonings; mix well.
— Cover. **Cook at 50% for 60 to 70 minutes, or until the meat is tender. Stir midway through cooking time.**
— **Allow to stand covered for 10 minutes. Serve.**

* Steps requiring modification are indicated in bold type.

Taking Full Advantage of Your Microwave: Meal Planning Made Easy

From the Freezer to the Table

Technological change and the hectic pace of modern life are constantly forcing us to change our ways of doing things and revise our already overloaded schedules. Time, work and leisure must all be carefully organized, and no tool is more useful to this end than the microwave oven. It can, in fact, quickly become indispensable, turning meals and their planning into virtual child's play.

Once you are involved in preparing something, doubling or even tripling the amount you make often adds very little to your preparation time. And just think how convenient you will find having the extra supply on hand. Consider a basic meat and tomato sauce, for instance—simple and inexpensive to prepare, and somehow even tastier when made in quantity, stored and reheated. Just divide the excess amount into meal-size portions and freeze in anticipation of those inevitable days when time or inclination to cook are lacking. Not only will you be pleased with the convenience, you will also find it easy to adapt this recipe to your fancy of the moment; you can serve it over pasta, use it to stuff a squash or pepper or as garnish for an omelette. As well, you can alter the flavor and/or consistency by adding a variety of ingredients—spices, vegetables, cheese, wine.

Everyone agrees: frozen food seems freshly cooked and retains all its original flavor when heated in a microwave. Moreover, potential savings are not limited to time—your budget will benefit as well. The speed with which food can be defrosted in the microwave will allow you to make more efficient use of your freezer, eliminating worries about overstocking. On the one hand, you can take full advantage of specials; on the other, you can quickly concoct a delightfully tasty dish from stored leftovers. Your social life, as a result, is bound to be more relaxed and pleasant. You need never again find yourself at a loss if friends turn up unexpectedly, nor need preparations for a dinner party keep you in the kitchen away from your guests. In other words, you can enjoy your company while your microwave does the work.

Of course, a degree of organization is necessary if you are to make optimum use of your appliance. So is careful attention to the general rules that govern the storage, defrosting and cooking of various foods. There are also a number of "tricks" and shortcuts that can make your task easier—freezing cooked and uncooked foods in containers that can go directly into the microwave, to mention just one. Not only is this a time-saver, it ensures maximum retention of flavor.

Planning Complete Meals

All too many owners of microwave ovens content themselves with using them for defrosting and reheating. This is a pity because a microwave can serve fully as well as a conventional oven for the preparation of complete meals—and take less time to do so.

Nor is any great expertise on your part required. Scheduling is really just a matter of common sense. Begin by cooking dishes that will be served cold. Next cook those that require longer cooking and standing times. Follow with the vegetables and, finally, with those foods that cook very quickly.

The small amount of effort you may initially have to put into adjusting your thinking and your ways to the use of the microwave will be richly rewarded. Cooking will be less of a chore. You will have more leisure time and be better able to relax and enjoy it.

Recommended Quantitities for Different Cuts

Cut	Amount per serving
Steaks and boneless roasts	115 g to 140 g (1/4 to 1/3 lb)
Rib roasts and braising cuts	140 g to 225 g (1/3 to 1/2 lb)
Round steak	140 g to 225 g (1/3 to 1/2 lb)
Cuts containing a lot of fat and bone (rump, short rib, shank)	450 g (1 lb)

Plan your meat purchases in relation to the number of times you foresee serving a particular cut and the number of servings per meal. For example, if you intend to buy enough ground beef to make three main courses for four people as well as a meat sauce, you will need approximately 2 kilograms. This kind of planning will allow you to avoid waste and ensure adequate servings. See the accompanying chart for recommended quantities per serving for different cuts of beef.

MICROTIPS

Searing Meat

Contrary to popular belief, it is possible to sear meat in the microwave oven.

Conventional cooking often calls for browning a roast before putting it in the oven in order to seal in juices and provide an attractive, well-browned appearance. A similar procedure, requiring the use of a browning dish, can be followed in the microwave. The bottom of the browning dish has a special coating that absorbs microwaves and so quickly gets very hot.

Preheat the browning dish in the microwave oven for about 7 minutes at 100%. Add butter or oil and heat for another 30 seconds. Without taking the dish out of the oven, place the meat in it.

Allow the meat to brown, then turn over to brown the other side. Cook according to the recipe instructions.

A Word of Warning

Never preheat the browning dish for longer than the time specified. A longer exposure to the microwaves might result in damage to the inside walls of the oven. Also, do not use the browning dish on a conventional stove; the coating could be ruined.

Freezing Beef

In the past, meat was commonly preserved by salting and drying. While these processes accomplished their primary function reasonably well, they were not an ideal solution to the problem of preservation since both flavor and texture were considerably altered—and not for the better. Fortunately for us, technology came to the rescue around the end of the nineteenth century when the first shipments of refrigerated meat arrived in Great Britain. Since then, preservation techniques have continued to improve so that today we can safely enjoy the full flavor of meat that has been frozen for months. A certain amount of care is needed, however, in preparing meat for the freezer.

Pay particular attention to how you wrap meat for freezing. The cold air of the freezer is extremely dry, and contact with it can cause meat to dry out and turn brown.

This is commonly referred to as freezer burn. It is also important to make sure that blood or meat juices cannot leak out of the package. The meat would lose not only moisture and flavor but also some of its nutritional value. Moreover, other items in the freezer could be affected, even ruined, if they came into contact with the meat juices. You therefore need wrapping that is watertight and airtight and that can be hermetically sealed.

Always make sure that the contents of a package, its weight, the date on which it was put in the freezer and the maximum time it may be stored are clearly indicated on a label that adheres to the package.

Easy-to-use freezer bags that provide a completely airtight seal are available in most supermarkets. If you don't have this type of bag, however, you may use

ordinary plastic bags and suck the air out of them with a straw.

It is a good idea to think ahead to the cooking process when you are preparing food for the freezer. Whenever possible, freeze meat or prepared dishes in containers that can go into your microwave oven. By moving directly from your freezer to the oven, you not only save precious time, you also reduce the risk of nutrient and flavor loss.

If you use ordinary plastic bags for freezing, remember not to transfer them to the microwave without removing twist ties that have a metal strip. Replace with plastic ties.

As to storage times, consult the chart on page 19, opposite, for guidelines in refrigerating and freezing specific cuts of beef.

Roasts

If you cannot vacuum-seal your packages, you can still prevent freezer burn by using plastic wrap that adheres to the surface of the meat.

Steaks and Patties

Pieces of waxed paper inserted between steaks or patties will make it easier to separate them for defrosting.

Cooked Dishes

Cooked dishes can be defrosted and heated in one operation by the use of a plastic bag placed inside a microwave-safe container.

Storage Times for Meat

Cut	Refrigerator	Freezer
Roasts	3 days	8 to 12 months
Steaks	3 days	6 to 9 months
Stewing Beef	2 days	6 months
Ground Beef	2 days	3 to 6 months
Offal	1 to 2 days	3 months
Cooked Beef	7 days	3 months

Wrap the meat well in the appropriate wrapping, which should be airtight and watertight, to avoid freezer burn.

Liver

To make defrosting easier, fold slices of liver before freezing them.

A Thousand and One Ways to Prepare Beef

We present here a mere handful from a multitude of justly celebrated beef dishes. These descriptions will help you decipher the jargon of menus and cookbooks. More importantly, they will also, we hope, provide you with ideas for creating variations on your own usual ways of preparing beef.

These dishes originated in several different countries or regions. Each one has its own unique, sometimes surprising, flavor. You will discover and delight in cuts of beef that are new to you, as well as in some basic sauces and garnishes that can serve as the inspiration for a wealth of others of your own devising.

Sirloin Florentine

Roast sirloin garnished with spinach dumplings and sometimes semolina cakes and served with a tomato-flavored demi-glace.

Amourettes Poulette

Slices of bone marrow poached in broth that has been flavored with herbs and served with a poulette sauce. Poulette sauce is a velouté of veal, mushroom essence and white wine, flavored with lemon juice and parsley.

Braised Beef with Gratin de Pommes Dauphinois

Beef braised in a white wine and demi-glace sauce, served with the strained sauce and a gratin de pommes dauphinois —sliced potatoes baked in a milk and egg sauce and topped with Gruyère cheese.

Beef Provençale

Beef braised in white wine and brown sauce with chopped tomatoes and garlic. May be garnished with mushroom caps stuffed with a garlic-flavored duxelles and sautéed tomatoes. A duxelles is a mixture of finely chopped mushrooms, shallots and onions, sautéed in butter, flavored with nutmeg and bound with heavy cream.

Beef à la Russe

Finely ground beef patties covered with a rich brown sauce to which sour cream is added. Grated horseradish and a little vinegar are also sometimes added. Usually accompanied by beets.

Beef Westmoreland

Roast beef served with a thickened gravy made from the drippings and may be accompanied by stuffed tomatoes, decoratively cut cucumber slices, green peas and potatoes roasted in browned butter.

Beef Tenderloin à la Forestière

Beef tenderloin roasted and garnished with morels and tiny bacon-flavored potato balls. Frequently served with Italian sauce, which is made with mushrooms, shallots, onions, tomato paste, white wine, ham, spices and parsley.

Mexican Filet Mignon

Garnished with mushrooms and red peppers and served with a very spicy tomato sauce.

19

Tournedos Rossini

Broiled filet mignon served on rounds of toast and garnished with slices of goose liver and truffles. Served with a Madeira-flavored demi-glace sauce to which truffle essence or chopped truffles may be added.

Beef Tongue Italian Style

Beef tongue, marinated and then braised in a light Italian sauce; may be garnished with artichoke hearts and noodles.

Braised Tongue with Currants

Tongue, braised or boiled and served with Madeira sauce flavored with a purée of currants.

Entrecôte Lyonnaise

Grilled sirloin or rib steaks served with a demi-glace sauce flavored with white wine, wine vinegar, sautéed onions and parsley.

Steak and Kidney Pie/Pudding

Cubes of stewing beef and kidney cooked with brown stock, onions and spices in, or topped with, pastry. May be baked or steamed.

Braised Oxtail à la Bourgeoise

Oxtail cut into uniform pieces and braised in light stock with root vegetables. The stock is thickened and served as gravy.

Vegetables to Accompany Beef

There is no doubt that, for the majority of us, meat is the central element of most main courses. It would be a mistake, however, to underestimate the importance of the vegetables that accompany and complement it. Thanks to their bright colors and varied shapes, vegetables can add a great deal to the eye-appeal of any meal at the same time as they provide us with indispensable vitamins, minerals and fiber.

As a result of rapidly improving communication, transportation and preservation technology, we have, over the past few decades, learned to appreciate a much wider variety of vegetables, and we are constantly discovering new ways of preparing and serving them. Some preparation methods are quite elaborate, others are simplicity itself. In either case, one thing is certain: there is no better way to cook vegetables than in a microwave. Because they cook from the inside, they do not dry out. And because very little water is needed, they retain all their color and flavor as well as their nutritional value.

Certain vegetables such as carrots, celery and leeks are sometimes added to beef dishes strictly for their flavor, along with herbs and spices, and are removed before serving. More often, however, these and other vegetables form an integral part of such beef dishes as pot roasts and stews—and who would deny that these flavorful blends of meat, vegetables and spices constitute some of our most appetizing and satisfying meals?

Cooked separately, an appropriate selection of vegetables can enhance the taste of meat, lighten a very rich dish or create a delightfully surprising contrast of flavor or texture. The flavor of the vegetables themselves may be enhanced by the addition of a single ingredient such as butter or lemon juice or complemented by a glaze, by spices such as ginger or paprika, by parsley or other herbs or by a variety of sauces ranging from a straightforward béchamel to a more elaborate hollandaise.

Most vegetables, moreover, adapt to almost any cooking method: braise, broil or steam them, stir fry them or bake them. Serve them puréed, diced, sliced or whole, alone or in whatever combination suits your fancy. The possibilities are infinite. You are limited only by your own tastes and your imagination— and to some extent by the meat dish the vegetables are meant to accompany. On this score, there are no hard-and-fast rules, but there are some general principles that can guide you in your choice.

If your main course is a rich one—Beef Wellington or a filet mignon with béarnaise sauce, for instance—you would do well to opt for a light vegetable such as parsleyed green or wax beans. A green salad will add a fresh and delicate touch to a hearty dish, such as stew or beef à la mode, that already includes some cooked vegetables. The sweetness of young peas or zucchini makes them ideal accompaniments to salty or highly spiced meats. A glazed or creamed vegetable, on the other hand, will go particularly well with a simply cooked meat course—a broiled steak or a roast beef *au jus,* for example.

MICROTIPS

Meals in a Minute

One of the great joys of the microwave oven is the possibility it provides of turning out a meal in minutes. A little bit of forethought is all it takes. Get into the habit of cooking two or three servings more than you need for any one meal. Divide the excess into individual portions and freeze or refrigerate in microwave-safe dishes.

Heated up in the microwave, these leftovers retain all their initial freshness and appeal. Indeed, they may taste even better than they did originally. Be sure, however, to cover them properly (with waxed paper or a lid) so that they do not lose any of their flavor.

Roast Beef with Herbs

Level of Difficulty	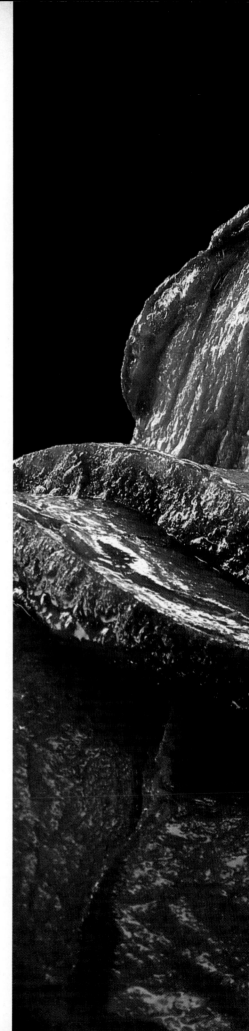
Preparation Time	10 min
Cost per Serving	$ $
Number of Servings	8
Nutritional Value	313 calories 34.5 g protein 4.5 mg iron
Food Exchanges	4 oz meat
Cooking Time	13 to 19 min/kg (6 to 8 min/lb)
Standing Time	10 min
Power Level	70%
Write Your Cooking Time Here	

Ingredients
1 1.3 to 1.6 kg (3 to 3-1/2 lb) beef roast
10 mL (2 teaspoons) parsley, chopped
2 mL (1/2 teaspoon) paprika
1 mL (1/4 teaspoon) oregano
1 mL (1/4 teaspoon) thyme
1 mL (1/4 teaspoon) rosemary
1 mL (1/4 teaspoon) garlic powder
1 mL (1/4 teaspoon) pepper
15 mL (1 tablespoon) Worcestershire sauce

Method
— Combine the parsley and other seasoning with the Worcestershire sauce; brush the roast with the mixture and place on a rack.
— Cook uncovered at 70%:
13 min/kg (6 min/lb) for rare roast beef;
17 min/kg (7 min/lb) for medium;
19 min/kg (8 min/lb) for well done;
or, using a temperature probe:
43°C (110°F) for rare;
49°C (120°F) for medium;
54°C (130°F) for well done; turning once halfway through the cooking time.
— Remove the roast from the oven and cover with aluminum foil, shiny side down.
— Allow to stand for 10 minutes.

Boneless Shoulder Roast

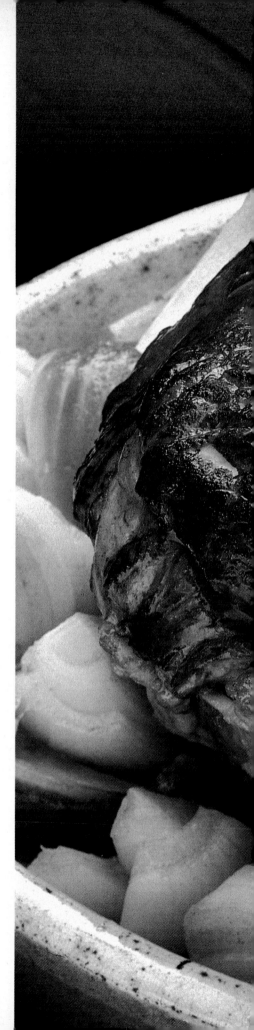

Level of Difficulty	🍴🍴
Preparation Time	15 min
Cost per Serving	$ $
Number of Servings	10
Nutritional Value	218 calories 40.9 g protein 5.2 mg iron
Food Exchanges	4 oz meat
Cooking Time	29 min
Standing Time	None
Power Level	70%, 100%
Write Your Cooking Time Here	

Ingredients
1 1.8 kg (4 lb) shoulder roast, boned
7 mL (1/2 tablespoon) steak spice
450 g (1 lb) salt pork, thinly sliced
375 mL (1-1/2 cups) strong tea
15 mL (1 tablespoon) cornstarch

Method
— Place the beef between 2 sheets of waxed paper and pound with a mallet.
— Sprinkle steak spice evenly over the meat.
— Roll up the meat.
— Bard and tie the roast and place it on a rack.
— Cook uncovered at 70%:
13 min/kg (6 min/lb) for rare beef;
17 min/kg (7 min/lb) for medium;
19 min/kg (8 min/lb) for well done;
or, using the temperature probe:
43°C (110°F) for rare;
49°C (120°F) for medium;
54°C (130°F) for well done; turn halfway through the cooking time.

⟹

Boneless Shoulder Roast

Assemble the ingredients needed for this recipe, which is particularly suitable for special occasions.

Arrange slices of salt pork over the roast.

Tie the slices of salt pork to the roast with string to keep them in place.

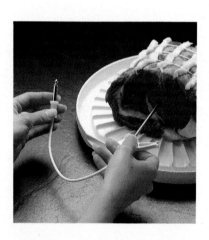

Place the roast on a rack and cook to your liking, with or without a temperature probe; give the rack a half-turn midway through the cooking time.

— Remove the roast from the oven, cover it with aluminum foil and set aside.
— Heat the tea for 2 minutes

Remove the roast from the rack and cover it with aluminum foil.

at 100%.
— Pour the tea into the rack and deglaze; add the cornstarch dissolved in a little cold water and cook

Deglaze the rack with the hot tea to recover the juices that have seeped out of the meat as it cooked.

for 3 minutes at 100%, stirring at one-minute intervals.

For Tastier Lean Meat

A number of beef cuts—including some of the more economical ones—are low in fat. Among these are the shank, blade, brisket plate and bottom round. While these are less tender than loin and rib cuts, they can be very tasty if cooked slowly with added fat, which serves both to keep them from drying out and to enhance their flavor. There are three basic ways to add fat to a lean piece of meat: you may bard, lard or interlard it.

Barding
A roast is barded by wrapping it in a thin layer of fat. The fat adds flavor to the meat at the same time as it preserves moisture by protecting the meat from the drying effect of the heat. A lean piece of beef that has been barded and cooked gently will be tender and delicious.

Larding
Meat is larded by inserting small strips of fat (salt pork, bacon, beef fat) into it. These strips, or lardons, melt as the meat cooks, providing both moisture and flavor. Larding is done by threading the lardons through a larding needle and pulling them through the meat. If you do not have a larding needle, you may make slits in the meat with a small, thin-bladed knife and push the strips of fat into them.

Interlarding
A piece of lean beef may be cut into slices which are alternated with thin strips of fat to provide more flavor and keep them juicy. This is known as interlarding.

A Few Tips
Follow the direction of the fibers when inserting lardons. By keeping the fibers intact, you avoid having the juices leak out and your meat will be more tender and flavorful.

You can vary the flavor of your meat by seasoning the lardons with parsley or other herbs or by marinating them first in a mixture of wine or spirits and herbs.

If you do not want anything to alter the flavor of your roast, use beef fat for larding.

The possibilities are many, and a pot roast can become an absolutely succulent dish if you lard the meat before braising. And it is such a simple operation . . .

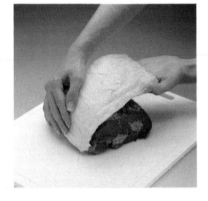

To bard a roast, simply wrap it in a thin layer of fat. This will keep it from drying out.

Inserted in a roast or pot roast, thin strips of fat called lardons melt as the meat cooks and keep it moist. This procedure is known as larding.

New England Braised Beef

Level of Difficulty	🍴
Preparation Time	10 min
Cost per Serving	$
Number of Servings	8
Nutritional Value	290 calories 30.25 g protein 5.5 mg iron
Food Exchanges	4 oz meat 1 vegetable exchange
Cooking Time	1 h 30 min
Standing Time	5 min
Power Level	50%
Write Your Cooking Time Here	✏️

Ingredients
1.1 to 1.3 kg (2-1/2 to 3 lb) corned beef
250 mL (1 cup) hot water
3 carrots, cut in sticks
2 potatoes, cut in quarters
1 cabbage, cut in quarters

Method
— Cut the beef into thick strips and place in a casserole.
— Add the water and cook for 45 minutes at 50%, stirring 3 times during the cooking.
— Arrange the vegetables over the meat.
— Continue to cook for 40 to 50 minutes at 50%, giving the dish a half-turn halfway through the cooking time.
— Allow to stand 5 minutes before serving.

The relatively low power level at which this simple recipe is cooked ensures perfect braising of all ingredients.

Cut the meat into thick strips.

After the first cooking cycle, add the carrots, potatoes and cabbage.

Give the dish a half-turn midway through the second cooking stage.

Beef à la Mode

Level of Difficulty	🍴🍴
Preparation Time	20 min*
Cost per Serving	$
Number of Servings	8
Nutritional Value	435 calories 35.28 g protein 4.5 mg iron
Food Exchanges	4 oz meat 1 vegetable exchange 2-1/2 fat exchanges
Cooking Time	1 h 55 min
Standing Time	5 min
Power Level	100%, 50%
Write Your Cooking Time Here	

* The meat should be marinated for 10 to 12 hours before cooking.

Ingredients
1.3 kg (3 lb) brisket point, cut in large pieces
2 pig's feet, split in two
10 2.5 cm (1 in) cubes pork rind
375 mL (1-1/2 cups) water
250 mL (1 cup) carrots, thickly sliced
125 mL (1/2 cup) onion, coarsely chopped
250 mL (1 cup) potatoes, cubed

Marinade:
175 mL (1/2 cup) red wine
45 mL (3 tablespoons) olive oil
75 mL (1/3 cup) onion, finely chopped
75 mL (1/3 cup) celery, finely chopped
1 bay leaf
1 clove garlic, crushed
15 mL (1 tablespoon) fine herbs

Method
— Combine all the ingredients for the marinade and add the pieces of brisket point and the pig's feet; leave to marinate in the refrigerator for 10 to 12 hours.
— Place the cubes of pork rind in a casserole, add 125 mL (1/2 cup) of the water and heat for 3 minutes at 100% to blanch.
— Remove the pork rind and set aside.
— Place the vegetables in the same casserole dish, cover and cook for 2 minutes at 100%; stir and set aside.
— Remove the beef from the marinade and place it in another casserole. Add the pig's feet and the pork rind.
— Strain the marinade, pour it over the vegetables and set aside.

— Add 250 mL (1 cup) of water to the meat, cover and cook for 60 minutes at 50%, giving the dish a half-turn midway through the cooking time.
— Add the partially cooked vegetables and the marinade, cover and cook for 30 minutes at 50%.
— Stir and continue cooking at 50% for 10 to 20 minutes or until the meat is cooked.
— Allow to stand for 5 minutes and serve.

MICROTIPS

To Defrost Ground Beef

To save time as well as to preserve all the flavor of ground beef, combine the defrost and cooking cycles whenever possible. To this end, use microwave-safe containers for freezing.

A ring dish is ideal for this purpose. Since there is no meat in the center where microwaves are less intense, the beef will defrost evenly. If the meat has been frozen in packages, divide the cycle into several stages. The first will allow you to separate the meat from its wrappings. After the second stage, scrape off the defrosted meat and set it aside. Break up the remaining frozen meat and return it to the oven for a third defrosting period.

Pepper Steak

Level of Difficulty	🍴
Preparation Time	10 min
Cost per Serving	$ $
Number of Servings	2
Nutritional Value	554 calories 55.3 g protein 6.6 mg iron
Food Exchanges	6 oz meat 5 fat exchanges
Cooking Time	8 min
Standing Time	None
Power Level	100%, 70%
Write Your Cooking Time Here	

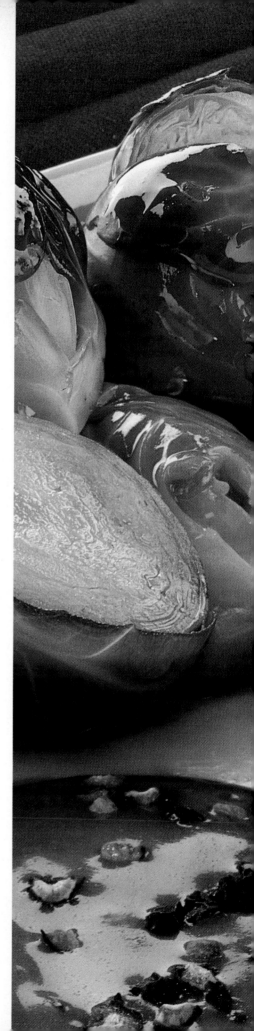

Ingredients
2 large T-bone steaks
freshly ground pepper to taste
30 mL (2 tablespoons) butter
15 mL (1 tablespoon)
browned flour
12 peppercorns, coarsely
crushed
125 mL (1/2 cup) 35% cream
30 mL (2 tablespoons) cognac

Method
— Pepper the steaks
  generously.
— Preheat a browning dish at
  100% for 7 minutes, add
  the butter and heat for 30
  seconds.
— Sear the steaks and then
  cook for 2 to 4 minutes at
  70%, turning them over
  halfway through the
cooking time. For a well
done steak, cook 2
minutes longer.
— Remove the steaks and set
  aside, covering them with
  aluminum foil, shiny side
  down.
— Mix the flour into the fat
  remaining in the cooking
  dish.
— Add the crushed
  peppercorns, cream and
  cognac.
— Cook for 1 minute at
  100% and beat lightly.
— Continue cooking at 100%
  for 30 to 60 seconds or
  until the sauce has
  thickened.
— Cover the steaks with the
  sauce and serve.

Steak with Tangy Sauce

Level of Difficulty	🍴
Preparation Time	10 min
Cost per Serving	$ $
Number of Servings	4
Nutritional Value	326 calories 30.9 g protein 5.2 mg iron
Food Exchanges	3 oz meat 1 vegetable exchange 3 fat exchanges
Cooking Time	15 min
Standing Time	2 min
Power Level	100%, 70%
Write Your Cooking Time Here	

Ingredients
1 450 g (1 lb) sirloin steak
60 mL (4 tablespoons) butter
4 onions, chopped
60 mL (4 tablespoons) flour
375 mL (1-1/2 cups) beef broth
50 mL (1/4 cup) cider vinegar
5 mL (1 teaspoon) sugar
1 bay leaf
1 mL (1/4 teaspoon) salt
60 mL (4 tablespoons) sliced pickles

Method
— Heat the butter for 30 seconds at 100%; add the onions and cook for 2 to 3 minutes at 100%.
— Add the flour and mix well.
— Add all remaining ingredients but the meat and stir.
— Cook for 6 minutes at 100%, stirring every 2 minutes; set aside.
— Place the steak on a rack and cook for 3 minutes at 70%, turning the steak over halfway through the cooking time. If the steak is still too rare after 3 minutes, cook a little longer at 70%.
— Let the meat stand 2 minutes, pour the sauce over it and serve.

To make the sauce, cook the onions in the butter, sprinkle on the flour and add remaining ingredients.

MICROTIPS

For Even Defrosting

When defrosting cooked food that includes a sauce or gravy, stir every once in a while so that the heat gets evenly distributed. Punctuate the defrosting cycle with a few periods of standing time. This prevents the less meaty parts and those more exposed to the microwaves from beginning to cook. Cover any defrosted parts with aluminum foil (shiny side down).

If time allows, let a defrosted roast stand for at least an hour before cooking. The meat will be juicier.

Steak with Madeira Sauce

Level of Difficulty	🍴
Preparation Time	10 min
Cost per Serving	$ $ $
Number of Servings	4
Nutritional Value	643 calories 60.9 g protein 7.96 mg iron
Food Exchanges	6 oz meat 1 vegetable exchange 2 fat exchanges 1 bread exchange
Cooking Time	12 min (+ 3 min for each steak)
Standing Time	2 min
Power Level	100%, 70%
Write Your Cooking Time Here	

Ingredients
2 large rib steaks, bone removed
125 mL (1/2 cup) celery, finely chopped
125 mL (1/2 cup) carrots, finely chopped
125 mL (1/2 cup) onions, finely chopped
45 mL (3 tablespoons) butter
45 mL (3 tablespoons) flour
375 mL (1-1/2 cups) beef broth
50 mL (1/4 cup) Madeira
1 mL (1/4 teaspoon) thyme
1 mL (1/4 teaspoon) savory
1 bay leaf

Method
— Cook the vegetables covered for 5 to 6 minutes at 100% in 50 mL (1/4 cup) water.
— Put the vegetables and their cooking liquid through the blender and set aside.
— Heat the butter for 30 seconds at 100%; add flour and mix.
— Add the puréed vegetables, broth, Madeira, thyme, savory and bay leaf.
— Cook for 6 minutes at 100%, stirring every 2 minutes; set aside.
— Cook the steaks one at a time on a rack at 70% for 3 minutes, or to your taste; to assure even cooking, turn each steak over halfway through the cooking time.
— Let the steaks stand for 2 minutes, cut into slices, then pour the sauce, reheated if necessary, over them and serve.

Assemble the ingredients needed for this quick, easily prepared dish.

After the vegetables are cooked, purée them in a blender (or put them through a sieve).

Cook the steaks one at a time on a rack at 70% for 3 minutes or more.

37

Sauces

For as long as people have been writing about food and cooking, special attention has been paid to sauces because of their ability to complement, enhance and even transform the food with which they are served. Whether accompanying a main course or a side dish, a well-prepared and appropriate sauce adds to the appeal of any meal. Sauces can be thin or thickened, simple or elaborate, delicately flavored or spicy, and a repertoire of basic sauces, along with an understanding of the possibilities for varying them, is one of a cook's greatest assets.

Faced with sauce recipes, inexperienced cooks are often intimidated by warnings of the dire consequences of a single misstep—lumpy béchamel, greasy gravy, curdled hollandaise . . . No need to worry anymore! The microwave oven has made virtual child's play of the preparation of most sauces. Moreover, sauces usually freeze well. Simply divide them into small quantities and store in individual microwave-safe containers. You can then transfer as much as you need directly from the freezer to the microwave for defrosting and heating.

Espagnole (Basic Brown Sauce)

A sauce made with a brown roux[1] to which rich, dark beef stock[2] and a mirepoix[3] are added, along with peppercorns and a *bouquet garni* (parsley, thyme, rosemary and bay leaf). Gently simmered and then strained, this sauce is the mother of all brown sauces.

Demi-Glace

Equal quantities of espagnole sauce and good strong beef stock, simmered slowly until reduced by half. In one variation, demi-glace may be flavored with Madeira and, in another, fresh tomatoes or tomato paste, meat trimmings and mushroom stems may be added, the mixture then being gently reduced, skimmed and strained.

Bordelaise

Demi-glace sauce flavored with well-reduced dry red wine, chopped shallots, thyme, bay leaf and black pepper. Butter is then beaten into the cooked and strained sauce for extra richness, and poached bone marrow and parsley are added just prior to serving. This sauce is traditionally served with grilled meat.

Duxelles

A classic sauce made by sautéing shallots and mushrooms in butter and adding white wine. After cooking to reduce the wine, tomatoes and a basic demi-glace are added, along with very finely chopped mushrooms that have been cooked in butter and parsley.

Hungarian

A white wine sauce flavored with sautéed onions, meat glaze[4] and paprika, to which sour cream may be added. A variation calls for chopped onions browned in butter, to which a sprinkling of flour is added, followed by a mixture of stock and meat glaze; this is then boiled and seasoned with paprika.

Piquante

Name given to a tangy brown sauce made with chopped shallots, white wine and wine vinegar; this is reduced and a demi-glace is added. The mixture is then strained, seasoned with cayenne pepper, tarragon and chervil and garnished with finely chopped gherkins and parsley.

1. Roux: A mixture of butter and flour that is used to thicken many kinds of sauces; its color depends on how long it is cooked.
2. Stock: A flavored liquid produced by simmering bones and trimmings of meat, poultry or fish in water with aromatic vegetables and herbs. A brown stock is made by browning the main ingredients before adding the water.
3. Mirepoix: A mixture of diced vegetables cooked gently in butter, sometimes along with ham or bacon and herbs; frequently used to flavor braised cuts of meat.
4. Meat glaze: brown stock that has been strained and reduced to a thick, syrupy consistency. Its flavor is so intense that very small quantities are used to flavor sauces.

Sauces and Soups, Volume 11 of *Microwave Magic,* will provide you with detailed instructions for making these sauces—and a host of others.

Blade Roast

Level of Difficulty	
Preparation Time	20 min
Cost per Serving	$
Number of Servings	10
Nutritional Value	367 calories 49.6 g protein 7.98 mg iron
Food Exchanges	4 oz meat 1 vegetable exchange 1/2 bread exchange
Cooking Time	2 h 30 min
Standing Time	5 min
Power Level	50%
Write Your Cooking Time Here	

Ingredients

1.8 kg (4 lb) blade roast, cut from the center
4 potatoes, cut in 5 cm (2 in) pieces
2 carrots, cut in 5 cm (2 in) slices
1 green pepper, cut in strips
1 Spanish onion, sliced
45 mL (3 tablespoons) flour
15 mL (1 tablespoon) brown sugar
2 mL (1/2 teaspoon) mustard powder
125 mL (1/2 cup) ketchup
175 mL (3/4 cup) hot water
30 mL (2 tablespoons) Worcestershire sauce
15 mL (1 tablespoon) vinegar
pepper to taste

Method

— Place the roast in a cooking bag; add potatoes, carrots, green pepper and onion.
— Combine all the other ingredients in a bowl; add the mixture to the meat and vegetables.
— Close the bag, leaving a small opening through which steam can escape.
— Place in a dish and cook at 50% for 2 to 2-1/2 hours or until the meat is tender, turning the dish every 30 minutes.
— Allow to stand 5 minutes before opening the bag and transferring to a serving dish.

After arranging the beef and vegetables in a cooking bag, pour in the mixture of the other ingredients.

MICROTIPS

For Even Defrosting and Cooking of Cubes and Meatballs

Whether you are defrosting or cooking, arrange the larger pieces of meat towards the outside of the dish where the microwaves are more intense. If the cubes or meatballs are all the same size, arrange them in a circle around the edge of the dish. Be sure to leave enough space between them so the microwaves can circulate.

41

Beef Flank

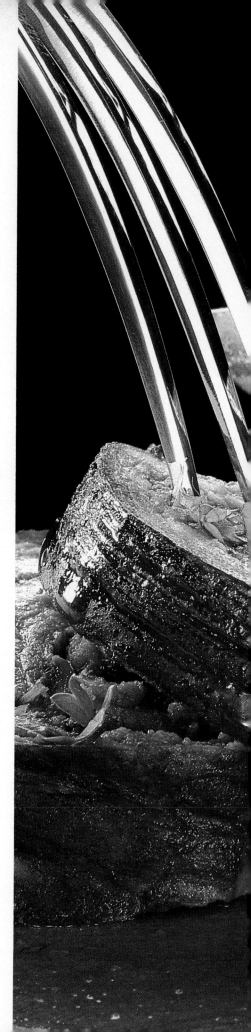

Level of Difficulty	🍴 🍴 🍴
Preparation Time	30 min
Cost per Serving	$ $
Number of Servings	6
Nutritional Value	330 calories Sauce: 200 calories 27.2 g protein 5.7 g protein 4.06 mg iron 1 mg iron
Food Exchanges	3 oz meat Sauce: 1/2 bread exchange 2 vegetable exchanges 1 vegetable exchange 1 fat exchange 3 fat exchanges
Cooking Time	1 h 5 min
Standing Time	5 min
Power Level	100%, 70%
Write Your Cooking Time Here	

Ingredients

1 large beef flank, cut in 3
1 small onion, finely chopped
450 g (1 lb) mushrooms, cleaned and chopped
2 mL (1/2 teaspoon) thyme
5 mL (1 teaspoon) chervil
2 mL (1/2 teaspoon) basil
2 cloves garlic, finely chopped
30 mL (2 tablespoons) chives, chopped
50 mL (1/4 cup) breadcrumbs
1 egg, beaten
salt and pepper to taste
30 mL (2 tablespoons) butter
22 mL (1-1/2 tablespoons) oil

Sauce:
75 mL (5 tablespoons) butter
30 mL (2 tablespoons) carrots, finely chopped
30 mL (2 tablespoons) onion, chopped
15 mL (1 tablespoon) celery, chopped
1 clove garlic, chopped
1 mL (1/4 teaspoon) basil
1 bay leaf
90 mL (6 tablespoons) flour
1.25 L (5 cups) hot beef broth
375 mL (1-1/2 cups) tomatoes, drained and chopped
125 mL (1/2 cup) dry red wine
salt and pepper to taste

⟹

Beef Flank

Assemble the ingredients needed for this outstanding recipe. It requires a rather lengthy preparation, but its exceptional flavor is sure to impress your guests.

Cut each piece of flank into two slices. Place them one at a time between sheets of waxed paper and pound with a mallet.

Stuff each piece, then roll it and tie with a string.

Method
— Put the onion and mushrooms in a dish, cover and cook for 3 minutes at 100%.
— Add the thyme, chervil, basil, garlic and chives; cover and cook for 2 minutes at 100%. Allow the mixture to cool.
— Add the breadcrumbs and egg; mix well and set aside.
— Carefully cut through the thickness of each piece of flank to get 2 slices.
— Place each slice between 2 sheets of waxed paper; flatten with a mallet.
— Season with salt and pepper.
— Place 1/6 of the stuffing on each piece of meat and roll; tie each roll with a piece of string.

— Preheat a browning dish for 7 minutes at 100%.
— Add butter and oil, and heat for 30 seconds at 100%.
— Sear the rolls in the browning dish; remove and set aside.
— To make the sauce, put the butter in a browning dish and heat for 1 minute at 100%.
— Add the carrots, onion, celery, garlic, basil and bay leaf.
— Stir, cover and cook for 2 to 3 minutes at 100%.
— Sprinkle with flour and mix well; add the beef broth and stir.
— Cook for 3 to 4 minutes at 100%, stirring halfway through the cooking time.
— Add the tomatoes, wine, salt and pepper.

— Cook for 1 to 2 minutes at 100%.
— Put the rolls in the sauce, cover and cook for 20 minutes at 70%.
— Reposition the rolls so that the ends facing the center are at the edge of the dish.
— Continue cooking at 70% for 15 minutes and rotate the rolls again.
— Cook at 70% for another 10 to 15 minutes or until the meat is cooked.
— Allow to stand for 5 minutes; cut the rolls into slices and arrange on a serving dish.
— Put the sauce through a fine strainer, pour over the meat and serve.

Sirloin Steak London Style

Ingredients
1 450 g (1 lb) sirloin steak
1 284 mL (10 oz) can beef consommé
15 mL (1 tablespoon) Dijon mustard
pepper to taste
15 mL (1 tablespoon) cornstarch
15 mL (1 tablespoon) water
30 mL (2 tablespoons) butter
300 g (10 oz) mushrooms, sliced

Method
— In a bowl, mix the consommé and mustard; add a generous amount of pepper.
— Add cornstarch dissolved in water.
— Cook at 100% for 2 to 3 minutes or until the mixture has thickened. Set aside.
— Preheat a browning dish for 7 minutes at 100%.
— Meanwhile, cut the meat into wide strips.
— Add the butter to the browning dish and heat 30 seconds at 100%.
— Sear the strips of meat and add mushrooms.
— Cover and cook for 2 minutes at 90%; add the sauce.
— Cook for 3 to 4 minutes at 90%.
— Allow to stand for 2 minutes and serve.

Level of Difficulty	▯▯▯
Preparation Time	10 min
Cost per Serving	$ $
Number of Servings	2
Nutritional Value	343 calories 50.6 g protein 9.2 mg iron
Food Exchanges	5 oz meat 1/2 vegetable exchange
Cooking Time	9 min
Standing Time	2 min
Power Level	100%, 90%
Write Your Cooking Time Here	

Beef Wellington

Level of Difficulty	
Preparation Time	20 min
Cost per Serving	$ $ $
Number of Servings	2
Nutritional Value	743 calories 52.2 g protein 9.33 mg iron
Food Exchanges	6.5 oz meat 3 fat exchanges 1-1/2 bread exchanges
Cooking Time	4 min
Standing Time	None
Power Level	90%
Write Your Cooking Time Here	

Ingredients
2 filet mignon steaks, 2.5 cm (1 in) thick
2 frozen sheets or rounds of puff pastry
100 g (3-1/2 oz) liver pâté
salt and pepper to taste
30 mL (2 tablespoons) melted butter
5 mL (1 teaspoon) soy sauce

Method
— Defrost the puff pastry.
— Cut each sheet or round in two and roll each piece as thin as possible with a rolling pin.
— Preheat a browning dish at 100% for 7 minutes; add 15 mL (1 tablespoon) melted butter and heat for 30 seconds. Sear the steaks and allow to cool completely.
— Place each filet on a piece of the pastry and cover with half the pâté; season with salt and pepper.
— Arrange the 2 remaining pieces of pastry over the filets, using any scraps for decorative motifs; brush the edges with a little water to seal.
— Add the soy sauce to the remaining butter and brush over the top.
— Place on a rack and cook 3 to 4 minutes at 90%, giving the dish a half-turn halfway through the cooking time.

Assemble the ingredients needed for this individual-serving version of Beef Wellington.

Divide each puff pastry sheet in two and roll out as thin as possible.

Place half the pâté on top of each steak.

Seal the pastry around the meat and brush with a mixture of soy sauce and butter.

Beef with Red Peppers

Level of Difficulty	
Preparation Time	15 min
Cost per Serving	**$**
Number of Servings	2
Nutritional Value	425 calories 47.2 g protein 7.3 mg iron
Food Exchanges	4.5 oz meat 1/2 vegetable exchange 3 fat exchanges
Cooking Time	4 min 30 s
Standing Time	None
Power Level	100%
Write Your Cooking Time Here	

Ingredients
340 g (12 oz) boneless blade steak
15 mL (1 tablespoon) oil
15 mL (1 tablespoon) butter
1 red pepper, cut in thin strips
175 mL (3/4 cup) beef broth
5 mL (1 teaspoon) soy sauce
pepper to taste
10 mL (2 teaspoons) cornstarch
10 mL (2 teaspoons) water

Method
— Cut the steak into thin strips.
— Preheat a browning dish for 7 minutes at 100%.
— Add the butter and oil and heat for 30 seconds at 100%.
— Sear the meat; add the red pepper.
— Cover and cook at 100% for 2 to 3 minutes, stirring once halfway through the cooking time.
— Add the beef broth, soy sauce, pepper and the cornstarch dissolved in water.
— Cook at 100% for 1 to 1-1/2 minutes, or until the sauce has thickened.

Assemble the ingredients needed for this quick easy-to-prepare recipe.

MICROTIPS

To Defrost Steaks

Remove as much of the wrapping as possible before beginning the defrosting. If the steaks have been stacked, separate them by inserting a knife-blade between them. As soon as possible, remove the rest of the wrapping. Turn the steaks several times, taking care to cover any defrosted parts with aluminum foil.

Always place the steaks on a rack for defrosting or on an upside-down plate set in a larger dish. Since liquids heat more rapidly that meat, it is important that the meat not sit in the juices that seep out of it. Otherwise, the parts in contact with the liquid might start cooking before defrosting is complete.

Since microwaves are more concentrated around the edges of the dish, arrange the steaks so that the thicker or meatier parts are at the edge. It is also advisable to give the dish a half-turn midway through the defrosting time.

Oriental Beef with Mandarins

Level of Difficulty	🍴🍴
Preparation Time	20 min*
Cost per Serving	$ $
Number of Servings	5
Nutritional Value	267 calories 25 g protein 6.6 mg iron
Food Exchanges	3 oz meat 1 vegetable exchange 1/2 fruit exchange
Cooking Time	7 min 30 s
Standing Time	None
Power Level	100%
Write Your Cooking Time Here	

* The meat should be marinated for 15 to 20 minutes before cooking.

Ingredients
450 g (1 lb) round steak
15 mL (1 tablespoon) soy sauce
125 mL (1/2 cup) orange juice
1 mL (1/4 teaspoon) ginger
1 clove garlic, crushed
15 mL (1 tablespoon) butter
15 mL (1 tablespoon) oil
500 mL (2 cups) broccoli flowerets
1 green pepper, sliced
1 onion, sliced
250 mL (1 cup) mushrooms, sliced
1 284 mL (10 oz) can mandarins, drained
10 mL (2 teaspoons) cornstarch
15 mL (3 teaspoons) water

Method
— Pound the steak to tenderize it; slice into 5 cm (2 in) strips, cutting against the grain of the meat.
— In a bowl, mix the soy sauce, orange juice, ginger and garlic.
— Pour this mixture over the meat and allow to marinate for 15 to 20 minutes.
— Preheat a browning dish for 7 minutes at 100%.

Oriental Beef with Mandarins

After pounding the meat to tenderize it, cut into narrow strips.

Pour the mixture of soy sauce, orange juice, ginger and garlic over the meat.

Remove the meat from the marinade after 15 or 20 minutes and drain thoroughly.

Add the broccoli, green pepper, onion and mushrooms to the seared meat.

Add the drained mandarins to the meat and vegetables; cover and set aside.

Pour the cooked marinade over the meat and vegetables.

— Add the butter and oil and heat for 30 seconds at 100%.
— Remove the meat from the marinade and drain; reserve the marinade.
— Sear the strips of meat in the browning dish, then add the vegetables.
— Cook 3 to 4 minutes at

100%, stirring once midway through the cooking time.
— Add the drained mandarins, cover and set aside.
— Dissolve the cornstarch in the cold water and stir into the marinade.
— Cook the marinade at

100% for 1 to 1-1/2 minutes or until it has thickened.
— Pour the marinade over the main ingredients, heat through at 100% for 1 to 2 minutes and serve.

Beef Surprise with Yoghurt

Ingredients
410 mL (15 oz) leftover beef stew
15 mL (1 tablespoon) onion
15 mL (1 tablespoon) butter
125 mL (1/2 cup)

mushrooms, fresh or canned (drained)
75 mL (1/3 cup) plain yoghurt
250 mL (1 cup) egg noodles, cooked
1 bunch of fresh parsley or

some flowerets of cooked broccoli

Method
— Put the onion and butter in a dish; cover and cook for 1 minute at 100%.
— Add the mushrooms, cover and cook 3 minutes at 100%.
— Stir, then add the beef stew; mix well.
— Add the yoghurt and mix well.
— Cover and cook at 90% for 3 to 4 minutes, or until the mixture is thoroughly heated.
— Spread the cooked noodles over the bottom of a dish.
— Garnish with the parsley or broccoli, then pour in the beef mixture.
— Heat for 4 to 5 minutes at 70%.

Level of Difficulty	🍴
Preparation Time	5 min
Cost per Serving	$
Number of Servings	3
Nutritional Value	446 calories 16 g protein
Food Exchanges	2.5 oz meat 3 fat exchanges 1 bread exchange
Cooking Time	13 min
Standing Time	None
Power Level	100%, 90%, 70%
Write Your Cooking Time Here	

Salisbury Steak

Level of Difficulty	🍴
Preparation Time	10 min
Cost per Serving	$
Number of Servings	4
Nutritional Value	463 calories 29.1 g protein 4.07 mg iron
Food Exchanges	3 oz meat 1/2 vegetable exchange 1 fat exchange 1 bread exchange
Cooking Time	12 min
Standing Time	None
Power Level	100%, 90%
Write Your Cooking Time Here	

MICROTIPS

Cooking with the Temperature Probe

The temperature probe can be used with many foods to assure the precise degree of cooking required. It is very simple to use; all you have to do is insert it in the food to be cooked and choose the appropriate cooking temperature. When the desired temperature has been reached, the oven will stop automatically.

Ingredients

450 g (1 lb) ground beef
1 carrot, grated
50 mL (1/4 cup) onion, finely chopped
50 mL (1/4 cup) celery, finely chopped
50 mL (1/4 cup) green pepper, finely chopped
1 egg
50 mL (1/4 cup) soft breadcrumbs
15 mL (1 tablespoon) Worcestershire sauce
15 mL (1 tablespoon) beef concentrate
4 slices of crusty bread
250 mL (1 cup) brown gravy

Method

— Place the vegetables in a dish, cover and cook for 3 to 4 minutes at 70%; leave to cool covered.
— In a bowl, mix the ground beef, egg, breadcrumbs, Worcestershire sauce and cooked vegetables.
— Shape 4 patties and brush them with the beef concentrate.
— Place the patties on a bacon rack and cook for 6 to 8 minutes at 90%; rearrange each patty so that the part nearest the center is at the edge and give the dish a half-turn after 2 minutes.
— Heat the gravy for 2 to 3 minutes at 100%, stirring once.
— Place one cooked patty on each slice of bread and cover with hot gravy.

Ground Beef Stew

Level of Difficulty	🍴
Preparation Time	20 min
Cost per Serving	$
Number of Servings	4
Nutritional Value	417 calories 39.7 g protein 5.7 mg iron
Food Exchanges	4 oz meat 1 vegetable exchange 1 bread exchange
Cooking Time	24 min
Standing Time	3 min
Power Level	100%, 70%
Write Your Cooking Time Here	

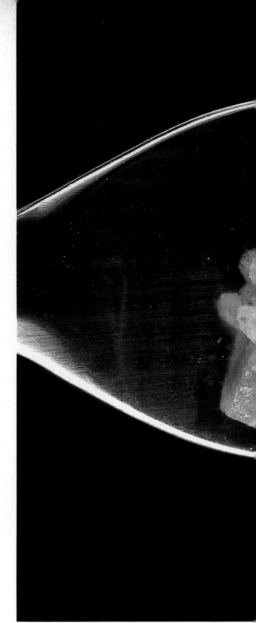

Ingredients
675 g (1-1/2 lb) lean ground beef
375 mL (1-1/2 cups) carrots, grated
250 mL (1 cup) celery, finely chopped
575 mL (2-1/3 cups) hot water
250 mL (1 cup) rice
1 envelope onion soup mix
1 bay leaf

Method
— Put the carrots and celery in a casserole and add 75 mL (1/3 cup) of the hot water; cover and cook 3 to 4 minutes at 100%.
— Add the ground beef and cook 4 to 5 minutes at 100%; interrupt the cooking time twice to break up the meat with a fork.
— Add the rest of the hot water and the remaining ingredients; mix well.
— Cover and cook for 5 minutes at 100%.
— Stir, reduce power level to 70% and cook for another 10 minutes.
— Remove the bay leaf, allow to stand for 3 minutes and serve.

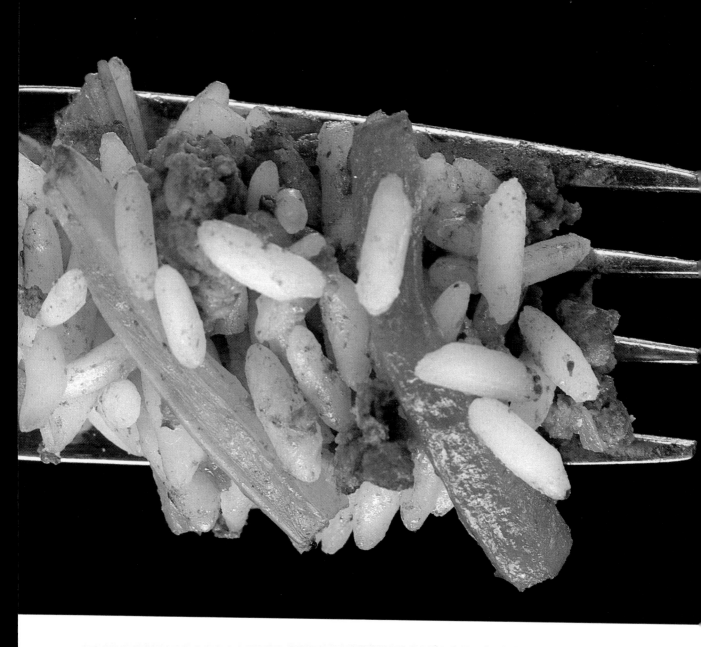

MICROTIPS

Preparing Meat for Freezing

In order to achieve the best results when freezing meat, always put it in a wrapping that is airtight and watertight. Contact with the cold dry air of the freezer would cause freezer burn and deterioration; at the same time, a leakage of juices would not only dry out the meat itself but might spoil other food.

The use of special freezer bags that provide an airtight seal is recommended. If you don't have this type of bag, use ordinary plastic bags, but suck the air out with a straw before placing in the freezer.

Make a practice of considering defrosting and cooking processes when preparing food for freezing. For example, when freezing a fairly large amount of ground beef, divide it into quantities of 450 to 675 grams (1 to 1-1/2 lb) and hollow out the center of each portion before packaging. This will make defrosting easier.

Meatball Kebabs

Level of Difficulty	🍴
Preparation Time	15 min*
Cost per Serving	**$**
Number of Servings	3
Nutritional Value	297 calories 32.7 g protein 5.1 mg iron
Food Exchanges	3.5 oz meat
Cooking Time	8 min
Standing Time	None
Power Level	90%
Write Your Cooking Time Here	✏️🍎

* This recipe includes a marinade that must be refrigerated for a few hours.

Ingredients
450 g (1 lb) ground beef
3 cloves garlic, crushed
1 hot red pepper, crushed
2 mL (1/2 teaspoon) ground ginger
5 mL (1 teaspoon) brown sugar
30 mL (2 tablespoons) soy sauce
60 mL (4 tablespoons) water
15 mL (1 tablespoon) fresh or dried coconut, finely grated
1 small egg, beaten
salt to taste
wooden skewers

Method
— In a bowl, mix the garlic, red pepper, ginger, brown sugar, soy sauce and water; refrigerate for a few hours.
— In a dish, thoroughly mix the ground beef, coconut,

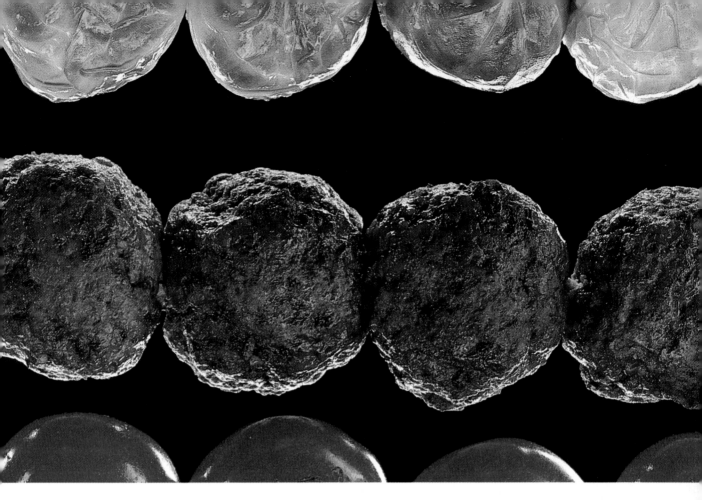

egg and salt.

— Shape the mixture into small, firm meatballs.

— Thread the meatballs onto the skewers; arrange the skewers over a dish, their ends supported on the sides of the dish so that the meatballs are not resting on the bottom.

— Cook 3 minutes at 90%.

— Brush the meatballs with the refrigerated marinade and cook at 90% for another 4 to 5 minutes, or until the meatballs are done.

— Halfway through the cooking time, rearrange the skewers so that those in the center are on the outside of the dish in order to achieve even cooking.

MICROTIPS

Bouquet Garni

A *bouquet garni* is made by tying together a bay leaf, two sprigs of parsley and one of dried thyme.

To Flour Meat

Put the required amount of flour and seasonings in a bag. Add a few pieces of meat at a time and shake. Use the leftover flour mixture to thicken the gravy.

Meatball Kebabs

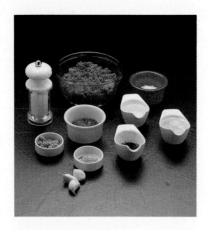

Pictured here are the ingredients you need to make this simple recipe, one that is sure to please.

Combine the marinade ingredients and refrigerate for a few hours.

Thread the meatballs onto wooden skewers and set over a dish, resting the ends of the skewers on the sides of the dish.

Cooking Utensils

Before rushing out to buy a new set of cookware for your microwave oven, make a thorough inventory of the dishes and containers you have on hand. Chances are that many of them can be used for microwaving.

The two main features to pay attention to are the material of which a dish is made and the shape. Any material through which microwaves can pass may be used: glass, porcelain, pottery, ceramic (providing there is no metal content); plastic that can hold hot food without losing its shape; cardboard and paper (brown or white paper bags should not be used for cooking); straw, wicker and

many others. Never use metal containers in your microwave oven. Metal reflects microwaves: not only would food in a metal container not cook, it would not even warm up and your oven might be seriously damaged.

Circular dishes are preferable since they allow for more even defrosting, heating and cooking than other shapes. Best of all is the ring dish because it has no food in the center. The corners of square dishes get double exposure to the microwaves, which causes food there to cook more quickly. Food in rectangular dishes also receives uneven exposure to the microwaves, twice as much in the corners

and little in the center. This is not to say, however, that such dishes cannot be used. It is simply necessary to stir or reposition the food more often during cooking and possibly to shield areas that will cook faster or to reduce the power level.

There are, on the other hand, two items that we strongly recommend to microwave users: the defrosting rack, which is designed to prevent meat from sitting in its juices since this might result in premature cooking, and the browning dish, which will allow you to give your meat an attractive golden-brown appearance.

Meatballs with Baked Beans

Ingredients
450 g (1 lb) ground beef
50 mL (1/4 cup) breadcrumbs
10 mL (2 teaspoons)
Worcestershire sauce

0.5 mL (1/8 teaspoon) garlic powder
75 mL (1/3 cup) onion, chopped
50 mL (1/4 cup) celery, chopped
1 796 mL (28 oz) can baked beans
50 mL (1/4 cup) ketchup
15 mL (1 tablespoon) molasses

Level of Difficulty	⑪
Preparation Time	10 min
Cost per Serving	$
Number of Servings	4
Nutritional Value	479 calories 34.1 g protein 8.45 mg iron
Food Exchanges	4 oz meat 1 fat exchange 1 bread exchange
Cooking Time	14 min
Standing Time	3 min
Power Level	90%, 100%
Write Your Cooking Time Here	✏️

Method
— Combine the ground beef, breadcrumbs, Worcestershire sauce and garlic powder; shape into small meatballs.
— Arrange the meatballs on a rack and cook 4 to 6 minutes at 90%, turning the dish midway through the cooking time; set aside.
— Put the onion and celery in a dish; cover and cook for 2 to 3 minutes at 100%.
— Add the beans, ketchup and molasses; mix well.
— Heat for 4 to 5 minutes at 100%, stirring once.
— Add the cooked meatballs and allow to stand 3 minutes before serving.

Moussaka

Level of Difficulty	
Preparation Time	30 min*
Cost per Serving	$ $
Number of Servings	8
Nutritional Value	464 calories 34.4 g protein 6.1 mg iron
Food Exchanges	4 oz meat 2 vegetable exchanges 2 fat exchanges 1/2 milk exchange
Cooking Time	59 min
Standing Time	5 min
Power Level	70%, 100%
Write Your Cooking Time Here	

* The eggplants must be salted and left to sweat for 2 hours before cooking.

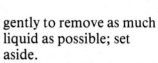

Ingredients
900 g (2 lb) lean ground beef
900 g (2 lb) eggplant
1 large onion, chopped
5 cloves garlic, finely chopped
1 540 mL (19 oz) can tomatoes, drained and broken up
250 mL (1 cup) tomato juice
2 mL (1/2 teaspoon) cinnamon
1 bay leaf
salt and pepper to taste
90 mL (6 tablespoons) butter
90 mL (6 tablespoons) flour
750 mL (3 cups) milk
4 eggs, beaten
125 mL (1/2 cup) Parmesan cheese, grated

Method
— Peel the eggplants and cut them into 1.5 cm (1/2 in) slices.
— Draw the bitter juices from the eggplants by covering one side of the slices with table salt and leaving for 2 hours.
— Rinse and dry the slices and arrange them in a dish; cook for 7 to 8 minutes at 70%, giving the dish a half-turn midway through the cooking time.
— Remove the eggplant slices and dry them once more with paper towel, pressing gently to remove as much liquid as possible; set aside.
— Put the onion and garlic in a dish and cook for 2 minutes at 100%.
— Add the beef and cook at 100% for 5 to 7 minutes, or until the meat is cooked, separating with a fork every 2 minutes.
— Add the tomatoes, tomato juice, cinnamon, bay leaf, salt and pepper to the meat mixture.
— Cook uncovered for 10 to 12 minutes at 100%, stirring halfway through the cooking time; set

aside.

— To make the béchamel
sauce, melt the butter for
1 minute at 100%; add the
flour and mix well.

— Add the milk and cook at
100% for 7 to 9 minutes,
or until the sauce has
thickened, stirring every 2
minutes.

— Layer the moussaka by
arranging half the
ingredients in the
following order: meat
sauce, beaten eggs,
Parmesan, eggplant,
béchamel sauce.

— Repeat with the remaining
half of the ingredients,

this time, however,
leaving the cheese until
last.

— Cover the ends of the dish,
if rectangular, with 2.5 cm
(1 in) strips of aluminum
foil.

— Cook uncovered for 18 to
20 minutes at 70%,
turning the dish twice
during the cooking time.

— Allow to stand for 5
minutes and serve.

Cheesy Beef Pie

Level of Difficulty	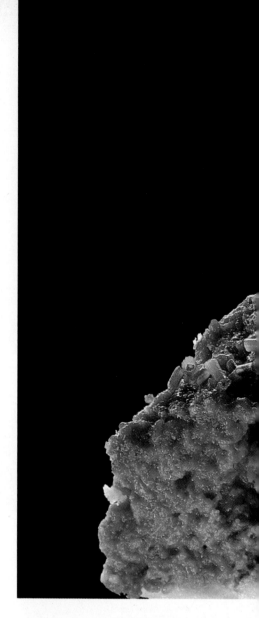 (utensils icon)
Preparation Time	10 min
Cost per Serving	$
Number of Servings	6
Nutritional Value	338 calories 20.8 g protein 2.09 mg iron
Food Exchanges	3 oz meat 1 fat exchange 1 bread exchange
Cooking Time	18 min
Standing Time	2 min
Power Level	70%, 100%
Write Your Cooking Time Here	

Ingredients
1 22.5 cm (9 in) pie shell
450 g (1 lb) lean ground beef
125 mL (1/2 cup) evaporated milk
125 mL (1/2 cup) ketchup
75 mL (1/3 cup) breadcrumbs
50 mL (1/4 cup) onion, chopped
3 mL (3/4 teaspoon) salt
2 mL (1/2 teaspoon) dried oregano
2 mL (1/2 teaspoon) pepper
5 mL (1 teaspoon) Worcestershire sauce
125 mL (1/2 cup) cheese spread

Method
— Pierce the pie shell with a fork and cook it, raised, on a rack, for 4 to 5 minutes at 70%, giving it a half-turn midway through the cooking time; set aside.
— Combine all the other ingredients except the cheese spread.
— Cook for 6 to 8 minutes at 100%, stirring once.
— Add the cheese spread, mix and pour into the pie shell; distribute the meat mixture evenly.
— Reduce the power level to 70% and cook for 3 to 5 minutes, giving the dish a half-turn after 2 minutes.
— Allow to stand for 2 minutes and serve.

Pierce the pie shell with a fork in several places so that it will not bubble up during cooking.

After adding the cheese spread to the meat mixture, pour into the pie shell.

During the final cooking cycle, give the dish a half-turn after 2 minutes in order to ensure even cooking.

Old-Fashioned Meat Loaf

Level of Difficulty	🍴🍴
Preparation Time	10 min
Cost per Serving	**$**
Number of Servings	8
Nutritional Value	279 calories 26.6 g protein 4.5 mg iron
Food Exchanges	3 oz meat 1/2 bread exchange
Cooking Time	14 min
Standing Time	4 min
Power Level	100%, 90%
Write Your Cooking Time Here	

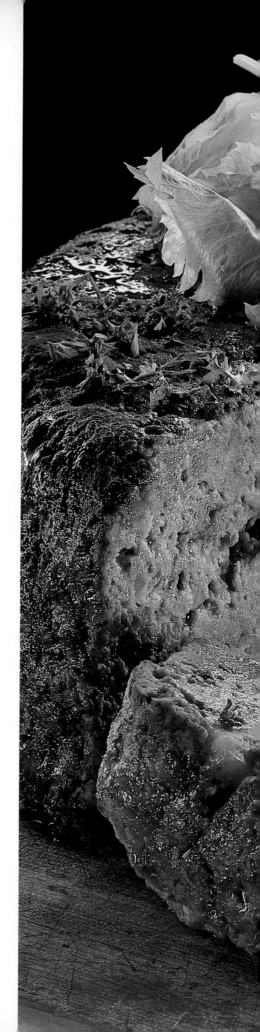

Ingredients
900 g (2 lb) ground beef
2 eggs
250 mL (1 cup) instant rolled oats
1 medium onion, chopped
250 mL (1 cup) applesauce
10 mL (2 teaspoons) salt
pepper to taste
2 mL (1/2 teaspoon) sage
15 mL (1 tablespoon) HP sauce

Method
— In a bowl, combine the ground beef, eggs, rolled oats, onion and applesauce; add salt, pepper and sage and mix well.
— Pour into a ring dish; make several small slits in the surface of the meat mixture.
— Brush with HP sauce.
— Cook for 4 minutes at 100%, turning the dish after 2 minutes.
— Reduce the power level to 90% and cook for 9 to 10 minutes more, turning the dish halfway through the cooking time.
— Allow to stand 4 minutes and serve.

Meat Loaf with Barbecue Flavor

Level of Difficulty	
Preparation Time	15 min
Cost per Serving	$
Number of Servings	4
Nutritional Value	411 calories 40.3 g protein 6.02 mg iron
Food Exchanges	4 oz meat 1 vegetable exchange 1 bread exchange
Cooking Time	25 min
Standing Time	None
Power Level	70%, 100%
Write Your Cooking Time Here	

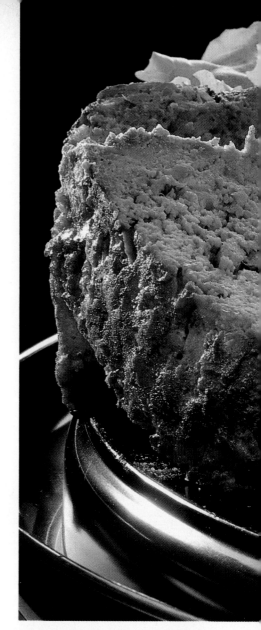

Ingredients
675 g (1-1/2 lb) ground beef
1 egg, lightly beaten
1 small onion, finely chopped
125 mL (1/2 cup) celery, finely chopped
1 package barbecue-flavored crumb coating
250 mL (1 cup) frozen green peas

Method
— Combine the ground beef, egg, onion and celery.
— Measure out 75 mL (1/3 cup) of the crumb coating and set aside; add the rest of the package to the meat and mix well.
— Put the meat mixture into a ring dish and sprinkle on the crumb coating that was set aside.
— Cook at 70% for 16 to 20 minutes or until the loaf is done, turning the dish halfway through the cooking time; set aside.
— Put the peas in a dish; cover and cook 4 to 5 minutes at 100%.
— Turn the meat loaf out onto a serving dish and fill the center with the peas.

Assemble the ingredients needed for this variation on traditional meat loaf.

Put the meat mixture into a ring dish.

Sprinkle the reserved crumb coating over the meat loaf.

Cook for 16 to 20 minutes at 70%, turning the dish halfway through the cooking time.

Steak Hunter's Style

	Single Recipe	Double Recipe
Level of Difficulty	🍴	🍴
Preparation Time	15 min	20 min*
Cost per Serving	$	$ $
Number of Servings	4	8
Nutritional Value	251 calories 61 g protein 13 mg iron	
Food Exchanges	4 oz meat 2 vegetable exchanges 2 fat exchange	
Cooking Time	14 min	21 min
Standing Time	5 min	5 min
Power Level	100%, 50%	100%, 50%
Write Your Cooking Time Here		

* Meat should marinate for 1 hour in the refrigerator.

Ingredients
Single Recipe
4 200 g (7 oz) sirloin steaks
1/2 clove garlic, chopped
30 mL (2 tablespoons) oil
15 mL (1 tablespoon) butter
340 g (12 oz) mushrooms,
thinly sliced
1 onion, thinly sliced
125 mL (1/2 cup) consommé
90 mL (3 oz) red wine
15 mL (1 tablespoon) tomato
paste
15 mL (1 tablespoon)
cornstarch
3 tomatoes, peeled and
roughly chopped
salt and pepper to taste
30 mL (2 tablespoons)
parsley, chopped

Double Recipe
8 200 g (7 oz) sirloin steaks
1 clove garlic, chopped
60 mL (4 tablespoons) oil
30 mL (2 tablespoons) butter
450 g (16 oz) mushrooms,
thinly sliced
2 onions, thinly sliced
250 mL (1 cup) consommé
150 mL (5 oz) red wine
30 mL (2 tablespoons) tomato
paste
30 mL (2 tablespoons)
cornstarch
6 tomatoes, peeled and
roughly chopped
salt and pepper to taste
45 mL (3 tablespoons) parsley

Method
— Add the garlic to the oil
and brush over steaks;
marinate for 1 hour in the
refrigerator.
— Sauté mushrooms and
onions in the butter for 2
(4-1/2*) minutes at 100%
and set aside.
— Combine the consommé,
red wine, tomato paste
and cornstarch. Cook at
100% for 2 (3 to 4*)
minutes, or until
thickened. Stir once
midway through the
cooking time.
— Put the steaks,
mushrooms and onions,

sauce and tomatoes in a
dish; cook at 50% for 5
(6*) minutes; stir and
cook for another 5 (6 to
7*) minutes.
— Season, allow to stand for
5 minutes, garnish with
parsley and serve.

*** Cooking time for double
recipe.**

MICROTIPS

To Peel Tomatoes

Simply place the
tomatoes in boiling
water for 1 to 2 minutes,
remove them and put
them in cold water. The
skin will then come off
easily with the help of a
small knife.

Marinated Steak

Level of Difficulty	🍴
Preparation Time	15 min*
Cost per Serving	**$**
Number of Servings	6
Nutritional Value	229 calories 33 g protein 5 mg iron
Food Exchanges	3 oz meat
Cooking Time	8 min
Standing Time	5 min
Power Level	90%
Write Your Cooking Time Here	🍎✏️

* The meat should be marinated for at least 1 hour.

Ingredients

1 kg (2.2 lb) round steak, cut into 6 pieces
1 medium onion, sliced
30 mL (2 tablespoons) ketchup
60 mL (4 tablespoons) lemon juice
zest of 1/2 lemon
60 mL (4 tablespoons) soy sauce
2 mL (1/2 teaspoon) thyme
1 bay leaf
125 mL (1/2 cup) water or consommé
15 mL (1 tablespoon) cornstarch

Method

— Prepare a marinade by combining the onion, ketchup, lemon juice and zest, soy sauce, thyme and bay leaf. Mix well and add the steak; leave to marinate for 1 hour at room temperature or overnight in the refrigerator.
— Stir the cornstarch into the water or consommé.
— Remove the meat from the marinade and set aside.
— Add the water or consommé mixture to the dish in which the meat was marinated to incorporate any remaining marinade and mix well.
— Immerse the meat in the liquid; cover and cook for 8 minutes at 90%; allow to stand for 5 minutes and serve.

Assemble the ingredients to marinate the steak for this unpretentious yet tasty dish.

Combine the ingredients for the marinade and let the steak steep in it for 1 hour at room temperature or overnight in the refrigerator.

Mix the cornstarch with the water or consommé to obtain a thicker consistency once it is cooked.

When the meat is well marinated, remove it and combine the water or consommé and cornstarch with any remaining marinade; mix well.

73

Beef Sausages

Level of Difficulty	 (fork and knife icon)
Preparation Time	5 min
Cost per Serving	$
Number of Servings	4
Nutritional Value	569 calories 20.1 g protein 2.22 mg iron
Food Exchanges	4 oz meat 4 fat exchanges 1 bread exchange
Cooking Time	15 min
Standing Time	None
Power Level	90%, 100%
Write Your Cooking Time Here	(apple and pencil icon)

Ingredients
12 beef sausages
340 g (12 oz) small potatoes, peeled
salt and pepper to taste
10 mL (2 teaspoons) dehydrated onion
2 mL (1/2 teaspoon) mustard powder
250 mL (1 cup) cheddar cheese, grated

Method
— Pierce the sausages with a fork in several places.
— Place the sausages on a rack and cook 4 to 5 minutes at 90%, turning the rack halfway through the cooking time. Set aside.
— Put the potatoes in a dish, drizzle the sausage drippings over them and season with salt and pepper.
— Cook covered at 100% for 5 to 7 minutes, shaking them twice during the cooking time; add the sausages.
— Mix the onion, mustard powder and cheddar cheese; spread over the sausages.
— Cook for 2 to 3 minutes at 90%.

Beef Tongue with Almonds

Level of Difficulty	🍴🍴
Preparation Time	20 min
Cost per Serving	$
Number of Servings	10
Nutritional Value	398 calories 27.7 g protein 3.1 mg iron
Food Exchanges	4 oz meat 2 fat exchanges 1 bread exchange
Cooking Time	1 h 37 min
Standing Time	None
Power Level	100%, 90%
Write Your Cooking Time Here	

Ingredients
1 large beef tongue
45 mL (3 tablespoons) butter
75 mL (1/3 cup) almonds, slivered
45 mL (3 tablespoons) flour
125 mL (1/2 cup) beef consommé, hot
60 mL (4 tablespoons) port wine
15 mL (1 tablespoon) tomato paste
5 mL (1 teaspoon) wine vinegar
pinch cinnamon
salt and pepper to taste
60 mL (4 tablespoons) 35% cream
parsley, chopped
750 mL (3 cups) boiling water, salted
30 mL (2 tablespoons) oil

Method
— Melt the butter for 40 seconds at 100%; add the almonds and cook at 100% for 2 to 3 minutes, or until the almonds are roasted, stirring midway through the cooking time.
— Add the flour and mix well.
— Add the consommé and port and cook at 100% for 1 to 1-1/2 minutes, or until the mixture thickens.
— Add the remaining ingredients except for the water and oil; cook for 1 minute at 100% and set aside.
— Place the tongue in a dish and cover with the boiling water.
— Cover and cook for 1-1/2 hours at 90%, turning the dish 3 times during the

cooking.
— Remove the membrane from the tongue and cut the meat into slices of equal thickness.
— Preheat a browning dish for 7 minutes at 100%; add the oil and heat for 30 seconds at 100%.
— Sear the slices of tongue and arrange them in a serving dish.
— Reheat the sauce, pour it over the slices of tongue and serve.

Assemble the ingredients needed for this original dish, one that will surprise—and delight—your guests.

Cook for 1-1/2 hours at 90% in salted boiling water.

Beef with Sliced Peppers

Level of Difficulty	▯▯▯
Preparation Time	20 min
Cost per Serving	$ $
Number of Servings	6
Nutritional Value	235 calories 28.9 g protein 4.5 mg iron
Food Exchanges	3 oz meat 1 fat exchange 2 vegetable exchanges
Cooking Time	13 min
Standing Time	5 min
Power Level	100%, 70%
Write Your Cooking Time Here	

Ingredients
675 g (1-1/2 lb) sirloin steak, cut in strips
75 mL (1/3 cup) soy sauce
30 mL (2 tablespoons) dry white wine or sherry
5 mL (1 teaspoon) instant beef bouillon powder
2 mL (1/2 teaspoon) sugar
2 mL (1/2 teaspoon) ground ginger
1 mL (1/4 teaspoon) garlic powder, or thinly sliced fresh garlic
pepper to taste
10 mL (2 teaspoons) cornstarch
30 mL (2 tablespoons) vegetable oil

1 large green pepper, cut in strips
1 large red pepper, cut in strips
4 green onions, cut in 2.5 (1 in) lengths
1 tomato, cut into eighths

Method
— Combine the soy sauce, white wine or sherry, bouillon powder, sugar, ginger, garlic powder and pepper.
— Add the cornstarch and stir to dissolve. Set aside.
— Heat a browning dish for 7 minutes at 100%; add the oil, being sure to spread it evenly; heat for 30 seconds at 100%.
— Sear the beef and stir until sizzling stops.

- Add the soy sauce
  mixture, the sliced
  peppers and green onions.
- Cook at 70%, stirring
  every 3 minutes, for 6 to 8
  minutes or until the
  vegetables are cooked but
  crunchy and the sauce is
  slightly thickened.
- Add the tomato and allow
  to stand for 5 minutes.
  Serve.

*This easy-to-prepare recipe will
please your most exacting
guests. Pictured here are the
ingredients you will need.*

MICROTIPS

Leftover Green Pepper

Any leftover green
pepper can be saved for
use in other recipes. To
store, dice it and freeze it
in a plastic bag. You can
use it later to enhance the
flavor of scrambled eggs,
soups and casseroles.

Beef Kidneys

Level of Difficulty	🍴🍴 🍴🍴
Preparation Time	25 min
Cost per Serving	**$**
Number of Servings	4
Nutritional Value	464 calories 21.7 g protein 11.66 mg iron
Food Exchanges	4 oz meat 3-1/2 fat exchanges
Cooking Time	22 min
Standing Time	4 min
Power Level	50%
Write Your Cooking Time Here	

Ingredients
2 beef kidneys, weighing a total of 1.1 kg (2-1/2 lb)
115 g (4 oz) lean side bacon
10 mL (2 teaspoons) parsley, chopped
15 or 20 mL (3 or 4 teaspoons) chives, chopped
2 green onions, chopped
1 clove garlic, chopped
pepper to taste
30 mL (2 tablespoons) spirits

Method
— Slice the kidneys lengthwise and cut into strips.
— Arrange the bacon in the bottom of a dish and add the kidneys.
— Add the parsley, chives, green onions, garlic and pepper.
— Cover and cook for 18 to 22 minutes at 50%, turning the dish halfway through the cooking time.
— Sprinkle on the spirits and allow to stand for 4 minutes before serving.

Assemble the ingredients needed for this recipe which is sure to delight kidney lovers.

Slice the kidneys along the length and cut into strips.

Arrange the strips of kidney over the bacon.

When fully cooked, sprinkle with spirits and allow to stand for 4 minutes before serving.

Italian Meat Loaf

Level of Difficulty	🍴🍴 🍴🍴
Preparation Time	45 min
Cost per Serving	$
Number of Servings	4
Nutritional Value	620 calories 48 g protein 6.7 mg iron
Food Exchanges	5 oz meat 2 vegetable exchanges
Cooking Time	14 min
Standing Time	5 min
Power Level	100%, 70%
Write Your Cooking Time Here	

Ingredients
675 g (1-1/2 lb) lean ground beef
125 mL (1/2 cup) breadcrumbs
450 mL (16 oz) tomato sauce
1 egg
5 mL (1 teaspoon) oregano
5 mL (1 teaspoon) salt
1/2 mL (1/8 teaspoon) pepper
375 mL (1-1/2 cups) mozzarella cheese, grated
10 mL (2 teaspoons) Parmesan cheese, grated

Method
— Combine the beef, breadcrumbs, half the tomato sauce and oregano, the egg, salt and pepper.
— Spread out on a piece of waxed paper, forming a rectangle approximately 1 cm (1/2 in) thick; sprinkle the grated mozzarella over the meat mixture and roll up, jelly roll fashion, with the help of the waxed paper; remove the paper.
— Place the roll in a dish and cook for 8 minutes at 100%; turn the dish, reduce the power level to 70% and cook for 5 to 6 minutes more.
— Heat the remaining tomato sauce and pour over the loaf; sprinkle with the rest of the oregano and the Parmesan cheese.
— Cover; allow to stand for 5 minutes and serve.

Beef Goulash

Ingredients
450 g (1 lb) lean ground beef
125 mL (1/2 cup) onion, chopped
1 796 mL (28 oz) can of whole tomatoes

500 mL (2 cups) zucchini, thinly sliced
375 mL (1-1/2 cups) macaroni, cooked
125 mL (1/2 cup) green pepper, chopped
1 156 mL (5-1/2 oz) can tomato paste

5 mL (1 teaspoon) sugar
2 mL (1/2 teaspoon) Italian seasoning
1 mL (1/4 teaspoon) garlic powder
1 mL (1/4 teaspoon) salt
pinch pepper
50 mL (1/4 cup) Parmesan cheese, grated

Level of Difficulty	⌇⌇⌇
Preparation Time	15 min
Cost per Serving	$
Number of Servings	4
Nutritional Value	401 calories 31.9 g protein
Food Exchanges	3.5 oz meat 2 vegetable exchanges 1 bread exchange
Cooking Time	21 min
Standing Time	5 min
Power Level	100%
Write Your Cooking Time Here	

Method
— Place the onion in a dish, cover and cook for 3 to 4 minutes at 100%.
— Add the beef and cook uncovered at 100% for 4 to 5 minutes.
— Separate the meat with a fork twice during the cooking.
— Add all the other ingredients except the Parmesan cheese; mix well.
— Cover and cook for 10 to 12 minutes at 100%, stirring every 2 minutes.
— Sprinkle with the Parmesan, cover and allow to stand for 5 minutes before serving.

Mexican Beef

Level of Difficulty	🍴
Preparation Time	5 min*
Cost per Serving	$
Number of Servings	4
Nutritional Value	441 calories 39.1 g protein 6.1 mg iron
Food Exchanges	5 oz meat 1 vegetable exchange 1/2 bread exchange
Cooking Time	10 min
Standing Time	None
Power Level	100%
Write Your Cooking Time Here	

* This dish has to cool before it is served.

Ingredients
450 g (1 lb) ground beef
1 onion, chopped
1 426 mL (15 oz) can kidney beans, drained
50 mL (1/4 cup) water
45 mL (3 tablespoons) taco seasoning
1/2 head of lettuce, shredded
2 tomatoes cut into eighths
250 mL (1 cup) white cheddar cheese, grated

Method
— Place the beef and onion in a dish; cover and cook at 100% for 5 to 6 minutes; separate the meat with a fork twice during the cooking.
— Add the kidney beans, water and taco seasoning.
— Cook 3 to 4 minutes at 100%; leave to cool.
— In a bowl, mix the lettuce, tomatoes and cheese.
— Combine the two mixtures and serve.

Grandmother's Macaroni

Level of Difficulty	
Preparation Time	15 min
Cost per Serving	$
Number of Servings	6
Nutritional Value	451 calories 26.3 g protein 4 mg iron
Food Exchanges	3.5 oz meat 1 vegetable exchange 2 bread exchanges
Cooking Time	15 min
Standing Time	4 min
Power Level	100%, 50%
Write Your Cooking Time Here	

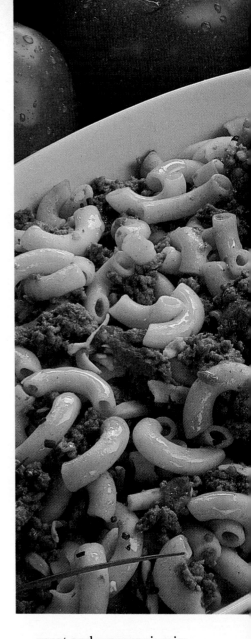

Ingredients
225 g (8 oz) ground beef
225 g (8 oz) maraconi, cooked *al dente*
1 796 mL (28 oz) can tomatoes
115 g (4 oz) cheddar cheese, grated
5 mL (1 teaspoon) sugar
2 mL (1/2 teaspoon) dried savory
5 mL (1 teaspoon) Worcestershire sauce
salt and pepper to taste
115 g (4 oz) cheddar cheese, thinly sliced
2 eggs, beaten
250 mL (1 cup) milk

Method
— Put the gound beef in a dish and cook 3 to 5 minutes at 100%; break up the meat with a fork halfway through the cooking time.
— Add the macaroni to the meat and set aside.
— Drain off and reserve 175 mL (3/4 cup) of liquid from the can of tomatoes; crush the tomatoes in the remaining liquid.
— Add the grated cheese, sugar, savory, Worcestershire sauce, salt and pepper to the crushed tomatoes.
— Pour this mixture over the meat and macaroni; mix well. Check the consistency and, if more liquid is needed, add the reserved tomato liquid in the quantity desired. Set the remainder aside for another use.
— Garnish with the slices of cheese.
— Combine the eggs and milk and pour over the macaroni and meat mixture without stirring.
— Cook for 8 to 10 minutes at 50% or until the cheese is melted.
— Allow to stand for 4 minutes and serve.

Assemble the ingredients needed for this old but enduring recipe.

Add the cooked macaroni to the meat.

Pour the tomato and seasoning mixture over the meat and macaroni.

Lasagna

Level of Difficulty	
Preparation Time	20 min
Cost per Serving	$
Number of Servings	6
Nutritional Value	604 calories 48.4 g protein 4.27 mg iron
Food Exchanges	4 oz meat 1 vegetable exchange 1 fat exchange 2 bread exchanges 1/2 milk exchange
Cooking Time	30 min
Standing Time	3 min
Power Level	100%, 50%
Write Your Cooking Time Here	

Ingredients
450 g (1 lb) lean ground beef
1 426 mL (15 oz) can tomato sauce
125 mL (1/2 cup) water
225 g (8 oz) uncooked lasagna noodles
500 mL (2 cups) ricotta cheese
750 mL (3 cups) mozzarella cheese, grated
125 mL (1/2 cup) Parmesan cheese, grated
parsley and paprika to taste

Method
— Place the beef in a dish and cook for 4 to 5 minutes at 100%, separating the meat with a fork twice.
— Add the tomato sauce and water; mix well.
— Spread one-third of the meat sauce in a suitable dish; using half at a time, add layers of noodles, sauce and ricotta.
— Mix the mozzarella, Parmesan and parsley; sprinkle over the lasagna.
— Cover and cook at 50% for 18 to 22 minutes, or until the noodles are cooked, giving the dish a half-turn halfway through the cooking time.
— Uncover, sprinkle with paprika and cook 2 to 3 more minutes at 50%.
— Allow to stand 3 minutes before serving.

Assemble the ingredients needed for this lasagna, which is not only delicious but economical and easy to prepare.

Cook the gound beef, breaking it up twice with a fork.

After alternating layers of sauce, noodles and ricotta, spread on the mixture of mozzarella, Parmesan and parsley.

Hamburger Quiche

Level of Difficulty	🍴🍴
Preparation Time	10 min
Cost per Serving	**$**
Number of Servings	4
Nutritional Value	419 calories 24 g protein 3 mg iron
Food Exchanges	4 oz meat 2 fat exchanges
Cooking Time	10 min
Standing Time	2 min
Power Level	100%, 50%, 70%
Write Your Cooking Time Here	✎🍎

Ingredients
225 g (8 oz) ground beef
4 eggs, beaten
125 mL (1/2 cup) green onions, chopped
75 mL (1/3 cup) milk
75 mL (1/3 cup) mayonnaise
2 mL (1/2 teaspoon) salt
pinch pepper
175 mL (3/4 cup) cheddar cheese, grated

Method
— Place the ground beef in a pie plate and cook for 3 to 4 minutes at 100%, breaking up the meat with a fork halfway through the cooking time.
— Make sure the meat is well broken up; drain and reserve.
— In a bowl, beat the eggs and add the green onion, milk and mayonnaise; season with salt and pepper.
— Pour the egg mixture over the ground beef; mix well.
— Place the pie plate on a rack and cook for 2 minutes at 50%.
— Using a fork, scrape the cooked mixture around the edge of the dish toward the center, allowing the uncooked liquid to run to the edge.
— Continue cooking for 2 minutes at 50%; sprinkle with the grated cheddar cheese.
— Cook at 70% for 2 minutes or until the cheese is melted and the center of the quiche is cooked.
— Allow to stand 2 minutes before serving.

These few ingredients are all you need to prepare this tasty yet economical dish.

MICROTIPS

Scrambled Eggs

Preparing scrambled eggs in the microwave oven is simplicity itself. Break 2 eggs into a microwave-safe bowl or glass cup and add 30 mL (2 tablespoons) of milk.

Beat with a fork and add 10 mL (2 teaspoons) of butter. Cook for 2 to 2-1/2 minutes at 100%, stirring at least once during the cooking. Let stand 1 minute to complete cooking and serve.

Beef in Patty Shells

Level of Difficulty	🍴🍴
Preparation Time	10 min
Cost per Serving	$
Number of Servings	4
Nutritional Value	283 calories 15.1 g protein 2.7 mg iron
Food Exchanges	1.5 oz meat 1 vegetable exchange 1 fat exchange 1 bread exchange
Cooking Time	18 min
Standing Time	None
Power Level	70%, 100%
Write Your Cooking Time Here	

Ingredients
225 g (8 oz) ground beef
4 7 cm (3 in) tart shells or 4 cooked patty shells
1 onion, chopped
125 mL (1/2 cup) frozen peas, thawed
2 zucchinis, peeled and sliced

Method
— If using tart shells, cook for 4 to 5 minutes at 70%, turning the dish halfway through the cooking time; set aside.
— Place the onion in a dish; cover and cook for 2 minutes at 100%.
— Add the ground beef and cook 3 to 4 minutes at 100%, breaking up with a fork midway through the cooking time.
— Add the peas and zucchini; cover and cook at 100% for 4 to 5 minutes, or until the vegetables are cooked.
— Pour the cooked mixture into the shells.
— Heat for 2 minutes at 100%.

This recipe, ideal for a first course or light lunch, can be made with either tart or patty shells.

MICROTIPS

Arranging Meatballs for Cooking

Large meatballs should be arranged in a cirle on a shallow 25 cm (10 in) round bacon rack. Smaller meatballs may be arranged in rows on a rack in a 30 x 20 cm (12 x 8 in) dish.

Beef Niçoise

Level of Difficulty	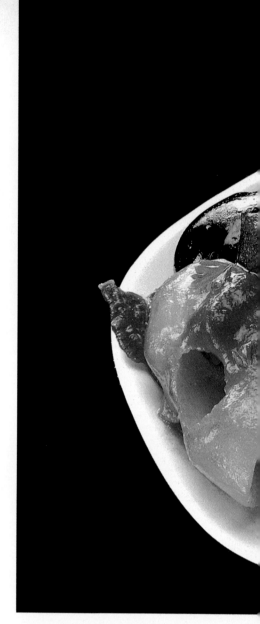
Preparation Time	25 min
Cost per Serving	$
Number of Servings	8
Nutritional Value	328 calories 32.4 g protein 5.25 mg iron
Food Exchanges	3 oz meat 1 vegetable exchange 1-1/2 fat exchanges
Cooking Time	44 min
Standing Time	5 min
Power Level	100%, 50%
Write Your Cooking Time Here	

Ingredients
900 g (2 lb) stewing beef, cut in 2.5 cm (1 in) cubes
115 g (4 oz) lean bacon
15 mL (1 tablespoon) oil
15 mL (1 tablespoon) butter
4 onions, sliced
2 cloves garlic, crushed
1 bouquet garni
45 mL (3 tablespoons) flour
250 mL (1 cup) water
250 mL (1 cup) red wine
30 mL (2 tablespoons) tomato paste
6 tomatoes, peeled and chopped
1 beef bouillon cube
salt and pepper to taste
15 mL (1 tablespoon) parsley, chopped
6 black olives

Method
— Cut the bacon slices into 4; spread out on a rack and cook 4 to 5 minutes at 100%; set aside.
— Preheat a browning dish for 7 minutes at 100%; add the oil and butter and heat for 30 seconds at 100%.
— Sear the beef cubes in the browning dish; remove and set aside.
— Place the onions, garlic and bouquet garni in the browning dish and cook covered at 100% for 3 to 4 minutes, or until the onions are translucent.
— Sprinkle with the flour and add the water and wine.
— Cook at 100% for 4 to 5 minutes, or until thickened, stirring every 2 minutes.
— Add the tomato paste, tomatoes and bouillon cube; mix well and season.
— Add the cooked beef cubes and bacon; cover and cook at 50% for 30 minutes.
— Stir and check the beef cubes for tenderness; cook

a little longer if necessary.
— Garnish with parsley and black olives; allow to stand for 5 minutes and serve.

Assemble the ingredients for this unusual dish which will add an exotic touch to your everyday menus.

Add first the flour, then the water and wine to the cooked onions and garlic. Cook until thickened.

Frankfurters and Beans

Level of Difficulty	🍴
Preparation Time	5 min
Cost per Serving	$
Number of Servings	4
Nutritional Value	480 calories 18.5 g protein 4.6 mg iron
Food Exchanges	3 oz meat 1 bread exchange 3 fat exchanges
Cooking Time	6 min
Standing Time	None
Power Level	90%
Write Your Cooking Time Here	

Ingredients
6 to 8 beef wieners
1 455 mL (16 oz) can pork and beans
1 small onion, diced
45 mL (3 tablespoons) ketchup
5 mL (1 teaspoon) prepared mustard
30 mL (2 tablespoons) dark brown sugar

Method
— Put the pork and beans, onions, ketchup, mustard and brown sugar in a dish. Mix well.
— Place the wieners, cut diagonally in 4 pieces, over the beans.
— Cover and cook at 90% for 4 to 6 minutes, or until the wieners are cooked.

Assemble the ingredients needed to prepare this quick, simple dish that is sure to please children.

Thoroughly mix all the ingredients except the wieners.

Cut each wiener diagonally in 4.

Place the wieners over the bean mixture, cover and cook 4 to 6 minutes.

Entertaining

Menu:
Spinach Salad
Salmon Vol-au-Vent
Beef Heart
Baked Potatoes
Fruit Salad

We all cherish the idea of entertaining family and friends with a casual and relaxed but nonetheless exquisite meal. And most of us, however well we have planned, end up going through agonies of uncertainty when the final moment of putting it all together arrives. Lack of time, lack of energy or lack of cooking experience make many of us hesitate to extend invitations as often as we would like.

But there is really no need for such hesitation. The menu we suggest here serves eight. It should convince you that it is possible for you to offer your guests a sumptuous meal with a minimum of time and effort.

As the main course, beef heart —a frequently underestimated and misunderstood meat— will no doubt surprise some of your guests. Preceded by a salmon vol-au-vent and accompanied by baked potatoes and a spinach salad, it is also sure to delight them. With a fruit salad to round out the meal, even the most demanding appetite will be well satisfied.

From the Recipe to Your Table

To ensure that a festive dinner for family or friends does not become an onerous chore, or even a major problem, begin by planning carefully. Preparing a complete meal in the microwave requires exactly the same kind of planning—no more, no less— as a meal cooked in or on a conventional stove. Only cooking and reheating times are different.

Order of preparation:
2 hours before the meal:
—Prepare the spinach salad and the dressing. Do not, however, add the dressing to the salad until just before serving.
1 hour and 40 minutes before the meal:
—Prepare the salmon sauce for the vol-au-vent.
1 hour and 15 minutes before the meal:
—Prepare the beef heart.
45 minutes before the meal:
—Prepare the fruit salad.
15 minutes before the meal:
—Cook the potatoes.
3 to 4 minutes before the meal:
—Heat the vol-au-vent sauce.
Just before serving the beef heart:
—Heat the heart cooking juices and pour over the meat.

Salmon Vol-au-Vent

Ingredients
2 213 mL (7-1/2 oz) cans
salmon
60 mL (4 tablespoons) butter
125 mL (1/2 cup) onion,
grated
60 mL (4 tablespoons) flour
750 mL (3 cups) hot milk
250 mL (1 cup) peas
250 mL (1 cup) carrots,
cooked and finely sliced
salt and pepper to taste
parsley to taste
8 vol-au-vent cases, cooked

Method
— In a dish, melt the butter
  for 1 minute at 100%.
— Add the grated onion and
  cook for 2 or 3 minutes at
  100%.
— Add the flour and mix
  well, then incorporate the
  milk and beat; cook at
  100% for 6 to 8 minutes,
  beating every 2 minutes.
— Add the salmon, peas and
  carrots and seasoning.
— Heat for 3 to 4 minutes at
  100%, stirring once.
— Serve in heated vol-au-
  vent cases.

Spinach Salad

Ingredients
500 mL (2 cups) spinach, torn into strips
250 mL (1 cup) cabbage, shredded
125 mL (1/2 cup) carrots, grated
50 mL (1/4 cup) onion, finely sliced
60 mL (4 tablespoons) mayonnaise
22 mL (1-1/2 tablespoons) vinegar
15 mL (1 tablespoon) honey
salt and pepper to taste

Method
— Mix the vegetables in a dish; cover and refrigerate.
— Prepare the dressing by combining the other ingredients.
— Pour the dressing over the vegetables just before serving.

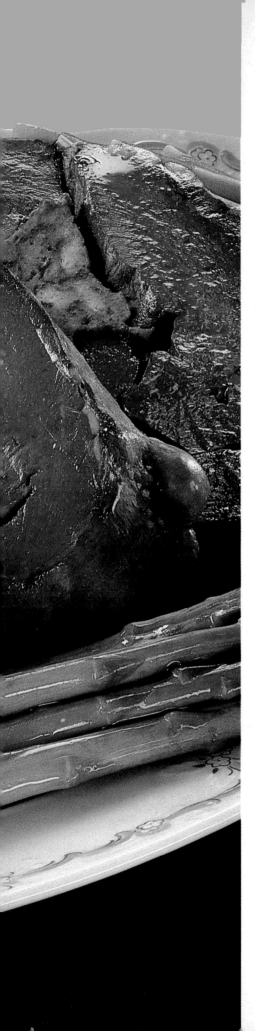

Choosing the Right Wine

At one time it was only in the rare (and probably wealthy) North American household that wine was served with meals. Over the past few decades, however, this situation has changed dramatically, and indications are that the consumption of table wines continues to increase. Certainly, few of us would now dream of planning a dinner party that did not include an appropriate selection of wines. And many of us appreciate the touch of elegance a glass of quite ordinary wine can give to the homeliest of meals. Even a hash made of yesterday's leftovers takes on a festive air when accompanied by a stemmed glass of ruby red, delicate rosé or golden white wine.

Along with our greater familiarity with table wines has come a greater self-confidence about choosing them, a greater willingness to trust our own tastes and to experiment. Nonetheless, remembering that the flavor of a wine can be affected, sometimes quite drastically, by the food that accompanies it (some fruity or vigorous red wines, for instance, take on a mildly unpleasant metallic taste in combination with fish or seafood), it is probably best to follow traditional guidelines when choosing wine for guests.

In general, you are unlikely to go wrong if you serve white wines with white meats, fish and shellfish. A light and delicate red wine that is low in tannin will also go quite well with poultry, veal and pork. The stronger, deep-colored and full-bodied reds are best served with red meats, their more pronounced flavor not being overwhelmed by the wine.

If you plan to serve more than one wine during a meal, begin with a younger, lighter wine and follow with a more mature, more robust one. Remember that some wines have a more complex taste than others. In order to emphasize the distinctive character of both the wine and the food, you may want to combine a complex wine with a simply flavored food—and vice versa. A young, fruity wine, for example, will go quite well with a sweet-and-sour dish. A fairly plainly cooked steak or roast, on the other hand, will be best accompanied by a medium- or full-bodied red such as a Rhône wine, a Bordeaux or a Zinfandel (a strong and fruity California red).

Stuffed Beef Heart

Level of Difficulty	🍴🍴🍴
Preparation Time	15 min
Cost per Serving	**$**
Number of Servings	8
Nutritional Value	427 calories 40.6 g protein 7.73 mg iron
Food Exchanges	4 oz meat 3 fat exchanges
Cooking Time	30 min
Standing Time	10 min
Power Level	100%, 70%
Write Your Cooking Time Here	

Ingredients
1 beef heart, 900 g to 1.3 kg (2 to 3 lb)
125 mL (1/2 cup) soft breadcrumbs
15 mL (1 tablespoon) parsley, chopped
5 mL (1 teaspoon) marjoram
zest of 1 lemon
nutmeg to taste
salt and pepper to taste
1 egg yolk
30 mL (2 tablespoons) melted butter
125 mL (1/2 cup) red wine

Method
— In a bowl, mix the breadcrumbs, parsley, marjoram, lemon zest, nutmeg, salt, pepper and egg yolk.
— Stuff the heart and tie it closed with kitchen twine so that it keeps its shape.
— Preheat a browning dish for 7 minutes at 100%; add the melted butter and heat for another 30 seconds at 100%.
— Sear the heart in the dish, then add the wine.
— Cover and cook for 28 to 30 minutes at 70%, giving the dish a half-turn and turning the heart over midway through the cooking time.
— Allow to stand for 10 minutes; cut the meat into slices; pour the cooking juices over the slices and serve.

Baked Potatoes

Ingredients
8 whole potatoes, washed but not peeled
120 mL (8 tablespoons) sour cream
40 mL (8 teaspoons) chives, chopped

Method
— With a fork, prick each potato in several places so that the skin won't split.
— Arrange the potatoes in a dish and cook uncovered for 10 to 12 minutes at 100%; give the dish a half-turn halfway through the cooking time.
— Cover the potatoes with aluminum foil, shiny side down.
— Let stand for 5 minutes.
— Meanwhile, mix the sour cream and chives.
— With a knife, make a slit in the top of each potato, squeeze to partially open and spoon about 15 mL (1 tablespoon) of the sour cream into the opening.

Fruit Salad

Ingredients
4 cantaloupes
1 L (4 cups) fruit of your choice (oranges, grapes, strawberries, cherries, blueberries) in any combination
250 mL (1 cup) kirsch

Method
— Split the cantaloupes into halves; remove the seeds; using a melon baller, scoop small balls out of the flesh.
— Fill the emptied cantaloupe shells with a combination of the balls and other fruit.
— Sprinkle with juice from the fruit and the kirsch.

Beef Terminology

Aromatic: Plant, leaf or herb with a strong and distinctive aroma, used to add a pleasant, subtle taste to dishes.

Ex.: saffron, chervil, tarragon, bay leaves, thyme.

Bard: To wrap lean meat in thin slices of fat before cooking in order to prevent the meat from drying out.

Bouquet garni: Herbs and aromatics (sprigs of parsley, thyme, bay leaf, savory, sage, celery, etc.) tied together for easy removal and used to flavor sauces, soups, stews and other dishes.

Braise: To cook slowly in a little liquid in a covered dish over a gentle heat in order to keep all the juices in the meat.

Clarified butter: The clear substance that remains after butter has been melted and cooled and the white, milky sediment at the bottom has been discarded. Thus treated, the butter stays fresh longer and can be brought to a higher temperature without smoking.

Deglaze: To pour a liquid (water, wine, cream, consommé, vinegar) into a dish in which meat has been cooked in order to dissolve the congealed juices so that they can be used to make a gravy or sauce.

Jus (au): Term used for meat served in its own cooking juices.

Lard: To insert strips of fat into lean meat before cooking in order to keep it from drying out and to enhance the flavor.

Lardon: Narrow strips of fat used for larding.

Marinate: To steep a food (meat, fish, vegetables or fruit) in a liquid to tenderize and/or flavor it. Meat may be marinated in oil and wine, vinegar, lemon juice or soy sauce, flavored with garlic, onions, parsley and other herbs, for example.

Marrow: The soft, fatty substance found in the cavities of beef bones. Marrow can be poached and served on its own or used in stocks and sauces.

Offal: Organ meats (liver, kidney, heart) and other parts of the animal often considered less than choice (tail, tongue).

Pot roast: A piece of meat, usually a less tender cut, browned and then gently braised in a covered dish.

Reduce: To boil a liquid to evaporate surplus liquid in order to enhance the flavor and produce a thicker texture.

Roux: A cooked mixture of equal quantities of flour and butter that is used to thicken sauces. It will be white, blond or brown, depending on how long it is cooked.

Scald: To heat a liquid to just below the boiling point.

Sear: To give meat an initial cooking in butter or oil at very high heat in order to brown it.

Season: To add salt, pepper and/or spices to food in order to enhance flavor.

Thickening agent: Any substance—such as cornstarch, egg yolk, roux—that can be used to give a thicker consistency to gravies, sauces and soups.

Truffle: A subterranean fungus that is greatly prized for its flavor and aroma. Because they are so expensive, truffles are usually used only in very small amounts as a garnish or to enhance the flavor of certain meat dishes, stuffings, pâtés and sauces.

Velouté: A white sauce made with white roux and a light stock that serves as the basis for many others sauces.

Culinary Terms

Have you ever been given a menu and found that you were unable to understand many of the words? Not only are there a number of culinary terms that are obscure but there are many ways to cook pasta or rice that have special terms to describe them. Here is a short glossary of terms with descriptions of their meanings that may help you.

Andalouse (à l'): Prepared with tomatoes, garlic, pimento and sherry.

Bercy: Prepared with shallots, butter and white wine.

Bolognaise: Prepared with ground beef and vegetables, mainly tomatoes.

Chasseur: Prepared with shallots, mushrooms, demi-glace, tomato sauce and white wine.

Colbert: Prepared with butter, lemon juice, nutmeg, cayenne pepper and Madeira.

Dauphinoise: Prepared with eggs, milk or cream and cheese.

Florentine: Prepared with spinach, onions and white wine.

Grecque (à la): Prepared with black olives, olive oil and lemon juice.

Italienne (à l'): Prepared with a duxelles of mushrooms and ham.

Lyonnaise: Prepared with onions, butter and parsley.

Normande: Prepared with apples, cream and calvados.

Occitane: Prepared with onions, tomatoes, garlic and salt pork.

Provençale (à la): Prepared with garlic, onions, olive oil, tomatoes, black olives and herbs.

Conversion Chart

**Conversion Chart for the
Main Measures Used in
Cooking**

Volume
1 teaspoon............ 5 mL
1 tablespoon......... 15 mL

1 quart (4 cups)....... 1 litre
1 pint (2 cups)....... 500 mL
1/2 cup............ 125 mL
1/4 cup............ 50 mL

Weight
2.2 lb.......... 1 kg (1000 g)
1.1 lb................ 500 g
0.5 lb............... 225 g
0.25 lb.............. 115 g

1 oz................. 30 g

**Metric Equivalents
for Cooking
Temperatures**

49°C............... 120°F
54°C............... 130°F
60°C............... 140°F
66°C............... 150°F
71°C............... 160°F
77°C............... 170°F
82°C............... 180°F
93°C............... 200°F
107°C............... 225°F

120°C............... 250°F
135°C............... 275°F
150°C............... 300°F
160°C............... 325°F
180°C............... 350°F
190°C............... 375°F
200°C............... 400°F
220°C............... 425°F
230°C............. 450°F

Readers will note that, in the recipes, we give 250 mL as the equivalent for 1 cup and 450 g as the equivalent for 1 lb and that fractions of these measurements are even less mathematically accurate. The reason for this is that mathematically accurate conversions are just not practical in cooking. Your kitchen scales are simply not accurate enough to weigh 454 g—the true equivalent of 1 lb—and it would be a waste of time to try. The conversions given in this series, therefore, necessarily represent approximate equivalents, but they will still give excellent results in the kitchen. No problems should be encountered if you adhere to either metric or imperial measurements throughout a recipe.

Index

MICROTIPS